# Re-energizing The Corporation

# Re-energizing
# The Corporation

*How Leaders Make Change Happen*

**Jonas Ridderstråle**
and
**Mark Wilcox**

JOSSEY-BASS
A Wiley Imprint
www.josseybass.com

# Contents

# About the authors

**Jonas Ridderstråle** (knightray@tele2.se) is at the forefront of the new generation of European-based business gurus. The Thinkers 50, a bi-annual global ranking of management thinkers, placed him (and his former colleague Kjell A. Nordström) at number thirteen internationally.

His uncompromising, imaginative and decidedly fresh take on contemporary business life makes him one of the world's most sought after and appreciated speakers. He acts as an advisor and consultant to a number of multinational corporations and helps run the Swedish Management Group – one of Scandinavia's leading management development companies. Jonas has an MBA and a PhD and is currently a visiting professor at Ashridge Business School in the UK.

Jonas' previous books *Funky Business, Karaoke Capitalism* and *Funky Business Forever* (co-authored with Kjell A. Nordström) are celebrated manifestos of how to make it in the new world of commerce, with global sales of close to 500 000 copies.

**Mark Wilcox** (Mark@RedThreadConsulting.co.uk) is the founder of the UK-based consulting firm, RedThread Consulting. Its clients include Sony, the British Army and Hilton Hotels. Prior to launching RedThread, Mark spent twenty five years working in the corporate world.

His career began as a maintenance electrician for Rowntree Mackintosh and then Nestlé. His work as a trade union representative led him to develop a passionate interest in training and development. He worked in various management development roles for Rowntree Mackintosh, Nestlé, the Albert Fisher Group and Cattles group of businesses. He then joined Sony Europe where he was responsible for talent development programmes and later became the Director of People and Organizational Development covering 9000 employees in 23 countries. Mark has an MBA from Bradford University, an MSc in occupational psychology and a degree in psychology.

# Introduction

## Re: Energized

This is how it started. Mark was running Sony's HR Development operations in Europe and Jonas was traveling the world talking about funky business, the title of his international bestseller (co-authored with Kjell Nordström). Jonas was brought in to kick-start a Sony event in Switzerland, *The Leadership Journey*. The aim was to galvanize a group of Sony's top executives into change. We also ended up galvanizing ourselves. This was the start of our own journey of friendship and working together over the next six years.

Truth be told, the Sony execs were a difficult audience. They had heard it all before. They *knew* they needed to change, but hadn't been energized into actually shaking off their skepticism and taking action. What we said made sense to them, but what next?

Jonas talked. He mapped out the trends impacting on Sony's business – the relentless rise of upstart competitors, the growth of the knowledge economy, increased expectations among customers for fantastic, tailored service. People were bewildered and inspired. And then, the executives separated into teams charged with various exercises to encourage them to look at the world in new ways.

Jonas stuck around and began to take notes. Mark was the conductor, creating the conditions on the journey to enable the participants to create their own sweet music – and save Sony money, generate new value, and inspire its future direction.

The event *was* energizing – more so than any previous corporate get-together that we had been involved in. We learned as much as the participants.

We realized that what we were talking about and doing were inextricably linked. The big picture world mapped out by Jonas benefited from the definition and the detail provided by Mark. And at Sony, our session led to real changes. More than 200 projects emerged from it. Over 250 million euros worth of change emerged. And, most of all, the managers began to take responsibility for their own challenges.

We knew we were onto something. Over the next few years we've continued to work together and with major organizations, exploring the dynamic and re-energizing interaction between the how and the why of change. *Re-energizing the Corporation* is the result.

It's a book based on real experiences with individuals and organizations. Since our initial re-energizing experience, Mark has become a consultant, helping organizations throughout the world tap into the change within them. Jonas continues to write books, articles and relentlessly travels the planet exhorting organizations to produce change. The *Why* and the *How* are still hard at work.

Why does this matter to you? Our personal experience mirrors a journey we see organizations undertaking throughout the world. Change is a fact of life. It's inescapable. Yet, too often, we come across individuals and organizations who believe they can escape. They have convinced themselves that change need not happen to them. Somehow – and we don't fully understand how or why – they believe that they are insulated against change. This is wishful thinking in the extreme. No one is immune to revolutions.

We remember running sessions for young students. We would go through the usual case studies, the management classics. Then we'd discuss the findings. Our students would often say that the crucial point in the case came about because: "The world changed . . ." Yes, the world does change. It's changing and will always do so. The choice is yours: reduce or produce change. In truth, there's only one choice.

This book aims to shake organizations out of their all too common torpor. It also intends to help those leaders who know they need to change to actually bring about that change through re-energizing themselves and their teams.

## About the book

*Re-energizing the Corporation* is unique. Look at the business book shelves and you'll find lots of big picture books that decoratively examine *why* individuals and organizations need to change. Alongside them will be a host of other books telling people and organizations *how* they should go about achieving change. This always struck us as weird and counter productive. To change, people and organizations need to understand both the why and the how. There's no mutual exclusion zone.

This is why this book is divided into two interlinked sections. Part One explains the big picture, the *Why*. This is Jonas' traditional domain. This section is focused on questions – the questions that you need to ask yourself in order to re-energize the future. Why is leadership critical to delivering change in business? Why is management no longer enough? Why do the talented people we all chase as employees demand so much more from their leaders? Why is it that doing better at what you've always done isn't necessarily going to secure your future? Why is re-energized leadership emerging as the critical distinction between seeing your growth curve turn down and those re-generating upward curves time and time again?

Part Two tackles the question of actually making change happen, the *How* of the equation. In order to do something you need to know *how*. This is where Mark brings his 25 years of corporate experience to bear in examining our model of change. How do the day-to-day actions of leaders impact on the delivery of organizational goals? How do the day-to-day actions of leaders deliver engaged people who want to make a meaningful contribution? How do leaders make sure that what they set out to do is achieved, time and time again? How do leaders ensure that the future of the company is secure and capable of constant innovation rather than simply maintaining business as usual? In essence: *How leaders make change happen.*

This section focuses on practicality. It's not a prescription for success but a tool kit of ideas, actions, suggestions, experiences of good and bad practice and lots of examples of how leaders go about the day-to-day reality of making change happen.

The two sections can be read separately, but we believe that the *how* and the *why* of change are linked. They are the conjoined twins of organizational life and need always to be thought of in relation to each other. Think Arnold Schwarzenegger and Danny DeVito in the movie *Twins* – unlikely and often uncomfortable bedfellows, but bedfellows nevertheless.

## Es of access

What links the sections together and our thinking as a whole is our $3^e$ leadership model. This is built around the three Es of Envisioning, Engaging and Executing:

**Envisioning**, the creation of a compelling shared picture of the future of the organization and its purpose;
**Engaging**, the building of a following of individuals who are committed to getting the vision into reality;

**Executing**, the delivery through teams of the outcomes that ensure your organizational vision is achieved.

This approach to leading change is rooted in common sense and emerged from experience and extensive research into what makes individuals and teams perform. It's both a philosophy about leading and a framework for action. As the Japanese say: "Action without vision is a nightmare; vision without action is a day dream."

An organization can use the approach in two ways: as a model of leadership development and as a model of project implementation. As you become more familiar with the framework you'll see, illustrated by vignettes and case examples, how re-energized leadership delivers change. It's this direct linkage that the model and approaches we advocate creates. Leadership for us is about making change happen; about moving from dreams to delivery.

Organizations are collections of people. This is obvious but the observation is often forgotten in the labyrinthian realms of management theorizing. History shows us that its people that determine the future of organizations, not their products or technology. Keeping people engaged with the organization has more future proofing power than any software or hardware updating program. People = Business.

Ask anyone who has worked at IBM over the last 10 years if they agree. Their old world dominance of mainframes was a great short term monopoly, which crashed when the PC came of age. Faced with competing in the cut-throat marketplace of small, standardized machines increasingly manufactured by someone else and plummeting margins IBM famously reinvented itself. What IBM did was to re-energize its people around a new business proposition, that of services and systems integration around e-business (on demand). Engaged with this idea IBMers were willing to do whatever it took to re-skill and reposition themselves.

The people who inhabit our organizations are calling out to be led, not managed, and certainly not micromanaged, as is the case in too many businesses. There are a lot of things that managers do that leaders need to also do, but they are never enough and they are rarely the things that inspire others to give their very best. Management only gets you so far; with re-energized leadership the possibilities are endless.

## Making a difference

Many traditional approaches to leadership focus on two dimensions, the management of people and the delivery of tasks. For years these two aspects of management have been charted on flip charts to show the need to balance the task with some form of respect for individuals. Other models show this relationship being complicated by the need to focus some attention on teams. All this is very necessary, but not sufficient if you're really to engage the brains and hearts, and therefore the real competitive advantage of the people, who work in your organization. As many business thinkers have said before, with every pair of hands you employ comes a free brain. It's the role of leaders to find ways to engage it.

This myopic tendency has created a school of thought in management development that concentrates on the delivery of projects or corporate objectives through the organization of team efforts. What's clearly missing from these models is some larger and in many ways more critical factor, the answer to the *why* question. Leadership, above and beyond the requirements of management, is about setting the agenda for the future, not just about delegating and scheduling resources to get things done. It's also about releasing the discretionary effort locked in every individual in the organization. More inspiration is required from the leader rather than perspiration by proxy. Leadership is fundamentally about change. If you're not leading change, then what *are* you leading?

Historically, thinking on leadership has reflected the science of the times. When leadership was all about warfare, and at least in Great Britain about class warfare, then it was related to the standing of the person in society, the breeding or bloodline that made them leaders. When the school of humanistic psychology started to gain influence in management in the 1950s and 1960s, leaders were considered products of their experience.

While thinking evolves to reflect our times, other debates rumble on. One of the longest running debates in psychology remains the question of nature or nurture. Most credible research seems to agree that our personality is influenced by both and offers a split decision on what has the most influence – our genes or our early experience. We believe that the same can be said of leadership ability. It's not really important to agree where the debate is settling now. What's more important is what works practically. Let's deal with practical measures and do whatever necessary to create leaders who provide organizations with the highest probability of success.

Of course, we agree that much can be taught to people about leadership styles and management techniques. However, it's clear to both of us and our colleagues in business that some people have much greater presence, greater drive and more ambition to lead. Failing to take notice of this fact and finding a way to determine it to some degree, is failing to maximize your business's chance of having great leadership talent.

We suggest you look for people who have existing positive strengths and then allow them to apply them. This is a much more positive approach to leadership. Work on the pluses not the minuses. Work on the *why* plus the *how*. By understanding and dealing with the *why* questions people ask you can then use the *how* methods to deliver a re-energized organization – one that has both the understanding of where it's going and why, as well as a way of getting there.

# Why + How = Energy

## The greatest

There has never been a more appropriate time for leaders to take up the challenge to do it well. Mohammad Ali, still a legend in the sporting hall of fame, once said: "If I had been a road sweeper I would have been the best road sweeper in the world, I would have been the greatest." We echo his sentiment. If you're going to step into the leadership ring, aim for greatness.

The time for management, command and control is past. Re-energizing leadership will be the real differentiator between successful organizations and those who only manage mediocre performance. In both the private and the public sectors there's a growing awareness that inspiring leaders are valued and rare animals who make a significant difference to the way people perform. Regardless of whether your mission is heart transplant operations at the most efficient cost and with the highest long term survival rate, or the dispatch of books to customers across the globe at the best price and shortest delivery time, leadership makes a difference.

And yet, time and time again, the effect an energizing leader can have on an organization is under-estimated. Leaders release the energy and discretionary effort of people. The leaders we see who are worth following, release the huge amount of latent energy that resides in the people that the organization has already chosen to work there. Their actions ensure that the organization has a healthy, vibrant pulse.

The leader determines the heartbeat of the organization. Flat line organizations don't attract or retain talent. Re-energized ones do.

**Jonas Ridderstråle & Mark Wilcox, September 2007**

# Acknowledgements

Writing a book is a team effort. A special thanks is therefore due to all the executives who have provided us with ideas, inspiration and interesting research material. You light our fire. Several business thinkers, consultants, speakers and academics have also been instrumental in influencing our view of the world of work. Some of these people are mentioned by name, others are just referred to as the thinkers behind research and particular studies. For a full list of references, please get in touch with either one of us.

British business writer and dear friend Stuart Crainer helped us in editing the book, honing our literary style and sharpening our arguments. As always, he greatly improved the readability of the text. For this, we (and all you readers) are most grateful. We're also deeply indebted to our professional publishers at Wiley. What a joyride.

Jonas wants to pay tribute to a bunch of other people more personally. His former colleague and partner in crime in three previous books, Kjell A. Nordström, has been instrumental in shaping some of the ideas present also in this volume. It has always been great fun to do stuff together – professionally and privately – "the vanilla gorillas will live on forever". Britt-Marie and Karoline at Speakersnet make gig-life both manageable and enjoyable. They never hesitate to help out with small and big things, at any hour of the day (and night). Thanks! Other speaker's agencies and reps throughout the world also play an important role in making business life truly pleasant. Zlatan, I have enjoyed the show so far but please make me cry with joy 2008 and 2010! Jan Lapidoth, all credit to you for persuading me to write books that people actually read. Jacqueline Asker, who does true wonders to ideas for new slides, is another critical success factor. Finally, a warm thanks to all colleagues at the Swedish Management Group (Mgruppen) and Ashridge. Just like family and friends you've been emphatic listeners as well as providers of valuable comments and support. I'm most grateful. Åsa, Joel and Siri, some time soon, a re-energized dad/husband will (re-)emerge from the shadows of our home-office. Promise!

Mark also has a few people to thank in name, either because they have given practical help and ideas or provided some kind of helpful intellectual stimulus. Writing this has required lots of both. This book wouldn't have been written without Stuart Sanderson, one of Marks's old professors at Bradford dispensing some of his wonderfully forthright wisdom. Had Mark not taken his advice to write a book he might still have been struggling with a PhD! On the journey there have been others who have helped in significant ways; Lucy Valentine for her contacts in publishing, Annie Medcalf, James Cullens, Roger Horrocks, Giuseppe Addezio and Roy White for their faith in methods and support when using them and Mark Jenkins, John McGee, Paul Sparrow and Dick Beatty for their valuable feedback on our ideas. Wider still Mark would like to thank two people in his early yeas who have inspired him and given him the confidence to do what he does. The first one is Malcolm Terry once tutor and early career colleague who inspired me to make a career out of learning and development. The second one is of course Rosemary Wilcox. Thank you for making me who I am and showing me the link between hard work and success. Thanks also to those closer to home who have lived with me as the book has evolved and given me the confidence to challenge and push on with it when it would have been so much easier to do nothing. So, massive thanks for the patience of Kath, Jo, Chris and Gary for tolerating me being at home more often and for making me proud of them in all that they do in their careers. I'm sure the next volume will be easier on everybody!

# PART ONE: WHY
## Re-energizing Thinking

# 1 Beyond the talent war

## The talent truce

Can you see the white flags of surrender – on both sides of the frontline? The war is over – for the moment. The war for talent announced early in the last decade has reached an unexpected end. The superstars of the organizational world suddenly realized that they need great organizations as much as these organizations depend on them. For most VIPs of commerce and competence, the ability to pick and choose turned out to be a figment of our collective imagination. A business world with only a limited number of corporations providing genuine "talent havens" did not result in unlimited choice for talent. As consumers, we've long known that any color so long as it's black is no real freedom. Now, as "competents", the combatants in the talent war, we can verify that truth. Bruce Springsteen was right; 57 Channels (and Nothin' On).

Talent needs Talent Inc. No matter how smart you are, you need other people to leverage your competence. Intellectual isolation isn't splendid. You need others because you're a social creature. As C.G. Jung once put it: "I need we to be fully I". In South Africa, people call this Ubuntu. You need others who you can love and at times loathe. We all crave colleagues who can provide us with that critical psychological boost. People need people.

Corporate leaders are also now beginning to realize that they can't survive without the celebrities of a competence-based business world. Talent Inc. needs talent. Today, wealth is created with wisdom. Successful firms rely on intellect inside. For the relationship between companies and talent to result in competitive advantages, however, it has to be exclusive. So, merely betting on the business brilliants who live in Free Agent Nation won't work. Corporations can't and shouldn't farm out the future to those mercenaries of competence who are willing to temporarily sign up to the highest bidder.

The result of the profusion of white flags is that organizations, as diverse as the Catholic Church and investment bank Goldman Sachs, now face the challenge of having to create places where talent wants to live and where ideas can happen.

Like any truce, the current one is fragile. As a leader, you're the guardian of it. Handle with care.

## Good news

The truce is great news for both sides. We're all winners. The best organizations will benefit greatly from nurturing talent and giving it an environment in which its full potential can be reached – and exploited. Yet, the truce doesn't mean that we've stopped competing for talent. Countries do it. Sports teams do it. Even opera houses do it. And corporations around the world most certainly do it. The reason is simple. Among the most eye-catching success stories of our times are energy-giving organizations built around talent. They and the people who hang around these force-fields are the true victors of the peace.

Think of it. The ideas and imagination of talented and motivated people are the sole success factor behind everything from Internet encyclopedia Wikipeda to Simon Fuller's *American Idol* on TV, from the super-innovative Chaos Pilot training-program in Denmark to Indian IT-service company Cognizant being able to boast more than 43 000 associates world-wide.

Ideas pay. A recent McKinsey report indicates that knowledge intensive corporations (organizations with more than 35% knowledge-workers) are more than three times as profitable per employee as labor-intensive companies. But, and this is perhaps even more interesting, in the former group of organizations, there's also much more variation in earnings performance. We've already warned you. Knowledge workers are fragile, and must be handled with care. They will want their piece of the pie and don't respond well to a Genghis Khan command and control leadership style. Talent requires positive energy to thrive. Star-power!

## Sustaining change

And now, the bad news. Organizations throughout the world find providing energizing environments in which talented people can reach their maximum potential incredibly difficult. And those that manage to create energetic environments often fail to sustain this energy. In the face of rapid, radical and revolutionary change, we're afraid that most great organizations will not adapt, alter course, astonish us with new, amazingly innovative products or services and continue to prosper. Instead, they will deny, deteriorate and die. D-daze is a fact of life.

As we write in 2007, neither the Greeks, Romans or the British rule swathes of the world. Nor are companies like IT&T and Digital Equipment still with us. Similarly, the Scottish post-punk band *Simple Minds* no longer show up on the radar screen of what's hot or what's up and coming. The next big thing has a habit of arriving and then disappearing, whether it be an invading army, a corporation or a rock band.

We shouldn't be surprised. After all, the natural law of free-market capitalism states that all sources of competitiveness are temporary. Call it economic entropy – over time each and every competitive advantage that we can come up with will, slowly but surely, evolve, erode and then disperse. The reality is that like snakes, under the pressure of competition, regions, companies and people need to shed their skin to be reborn and live on.

## More good news

Change isn't an impossible dream, however. It can be done. Think back to 1987 when the US President Ronald Reagan was besieged with problems. The Iran-Contra scandal was at its height. The one-time actor suddenly looked out of his depth, an innocent in a world of vipers. Then, in West Berlin, in front of a crowd of 40 000 people, he said: "Mr. Gorbachev, tear down this wall!" It was an historical moment and one which reversed the decline in Reagan's standing. Instead of appearing deeply troubled, he was the charismatic harbinger of a brave new dawn. While most experts were convinced that co-existence under a permanent balance of terror was constant, Ronnie was naïve enough to believe that change was possible. Indeed, it was and still is. His dream came true.

Or, for a more recent miracle, think about one time US Vice President and character of the cartoon sitcom *Futurama*, Al Gore, on his current quest to save the planet. Even stiff and emotionless people can become stylish and popular if they chose to re-create themselves; from eternal loser – to eternal cruiser. Grow a beard and see the world anew.

Look around. The greats, in whatever field, have an appetite for re-invention. Think of Miles Davis churning out the hardest funk when he was near the end of his life. Think of Picasso flitting from fashion to fashion, one brush stroke ahead of the artistic crowd. The British football team Manchester United has made a series of comebacks since many of its young players, labeled the Busby Babes, were killed in a tragic accident outside Munich back in 1958. Think again. For over three decades, pop-star and fashion-icon Madonna has constantly re-energized herself – artistically and personally. She is the definitive chameleon.

## This time – it's personal

Change is no longer what happens to other people, other organizations, at different times. Change is what happens to you and your organization, today and tomorrow. Change is personal and, even more good news, you can make a difference! Whether you're the CEO of a Japanese Fortune 500 company, a school-teacher in Serbia, a football coach in Argentina, an Indian IT-entrepreneur, or just plain old you, doesn't really matter. People *are* the decisive factor – in society, sports and business.

Commerce and change is now about so much more than land and raw-materials, sophisticated machinery and financial capital. Just as everything mankind has ever done, and still does, has an enormous impact on life on our planet, all the things energizing leaders now do have an enormous impact on the well-being of our corporations and on organizational life.

Times change. People used to be referred to as *labor*, an insignificant but annoying production factor. Sometimes, under the influence of some strange socialist opiate, we protested, went on strike, threatened and cajoled, but usually, we behaved. As labor fell into line, physical capital – in the form of minerals, oil-wells, forests and fields – was the thing that wealth was weaved of. The money was in mines not minds.

Now, the future is at once both lighter and brighter. For sure, the price of oil is up, so are copper, zinc and nickel, to name but a few commodities. But, even so, the average raw material is still only worth about 20–40% of what it was valued at 200 years ago. Even Russian President Vladimir Putin, a man currently heavily reliant on the hard stuff, argues that in the long term, the future of his country is more dependent on having the right soil for growing talent than having the ability to pump up more oil. Soil not oil. Raw talent is renewable, most raw materials aren't.

There was a gap between the days when commodities ruled and today's brain-led economies. After we stopped being so physical, financial capital became the great bean feast. You made money by having money and by mastering the art of managing money – from J.P. Morgan to Gordon Gecko. While we know that some of the Wall-Street-shufflers still make mega millions, compare their hills of beans to the personal wealth of the world's richest man, His Nerdship, Bill Gates. On Monday June 4, 2007 he was worth approximately $ 72 379 346 billion. The reality of our times is that there's an amazing abundance of capital and a genuine shortage of people who make competences happen and organizations that enable them to do so.

## Beyond the beans

Today, all the traditional stuff – extracting the oil and counting the beans – has become necessary, but no longer sufficient for the creation of sustainable competitiveness. The only thing we're left to compete with is 1.3 kilograms of brain multiplied by the number of people in our network. And this is true whether you're a band, a brand, a company or a country.

Take a step back and think about the amazing developments of the last few decades. Back in 1984, the same year that Prince issued *Purple Rain*, some 20% of the approximately 300 000 people who worked for the king of heavy, General Electric, were so called knowledge-workers. About 20 years later, GE still employs roughly the same number of people, but these days something like 55% of them are knowledge workers (and Prince gives away his albums for free). King Kong has gone soft, because these days the soft stuff is the hard stuff.

General Electric isn't alone. Research by the McKinsey Technology Initiative reveals that in the US around 40% of the labor force is now made up of people who have to solve complex problems. In this part of the world, close to three-quarters of all the jobs created during the last decade require considerable abstract thinking and judgment skills.

The pay-off is clear. None of this is an indulgence. Competent people translate into profits. Fact. If you know how to lead and energize them, brilliant people = fantastic pay-offs. Raise the white flag, now.

# 2  Come together

## The people's business principles

Without barricades being erected, the revolution has happened. People potentially rule. For better and for worse, your own talent and that of your fellow competents make all the difference in today's economy. Welcome to the You-volution! This time, it's all about you. Anita Roddick, founder of the Body Shop, once said: "If you think you're too insignificant to make a difference, try sleeping with a mosquito in the room." You matter.

Here's the next piece of good news. While change always starts with the individual, you're not alone. We've moved from Buck Owens' *Only You* to Lennon and McCartney's *Come Together*. Thanks to innovative technological platforms, entirely new Egos United networks have been opened up from Aalborg to Zagreb.

The most obvious such platform is the Internet. The birth and growth of the Internet means that YOU and others with a shared purpose can link up without the help of THEM. "We are entering a participation age . . . where the end points are starting to inform the center," says Jonathan Schwartz, CEO of Sun Microsystems.

With the pen, communication used to be one-to-one. Then, with radio and TV it became one-to-many. Today, with the Internet it's *all-to-all*. It's infectious. We're all active transmitters and receivers.

No one is formally in charge, but we can all potentially take charge. And boy, are many of us passionate about doing this kind of volunteer work. User-generated content phenomenon Wikipedia offers close to 5 million articles in more than 125 languages. Some 67 000 volunteers around the world contribute with editing and content. South Korean news site OhMyNews gets 75% of its content from a network made up of 40 000 of its readers.

One of the high points of the You-volution came in October 2006 when Google acquired on-line video company YouTube for $1.65 billion. Now, that's a lot of money when you consider that the company was started a little more than a year earlier by the late 20-somethings Chad Hurley and Steve Chen in Chad's (Mr. Hurley by now, we presume?) garage. At the time of the takeover, YouTube had 67 employees located at its office above a pizza restaurant.

The company kept the location. More importantly, however, before the acquisition Chad and Steve had attracted a loyal following of 20 million consumers like you and us who viewed videos, ranging from short home videos to clips recorded from TV shows, created by the likes of you and us – at a rate of 65 000 new uploads every day. YouTube succeeded by providing its users with the purpose and platform that enabled people to participate passionately in building the company for Chad and Steve and everyone else.

**People + Purpose + Platform + Participation + Passion = Profits**

## Generation choice

YOU RULE! Think about it. Over 110 million of YOUs created MySpace. Remember that the only organization that has been able to truly challenge Microsoft is Linux with its self-organizing system firmly based on the YOU-principle. Firms like Sun, Oracle and the rest of the US posse out to get Bill Gates had billions of dollars, but it was thousands of US who did it.

Think eBay. The company brokers in the excess of 50 billion auction transactions a year, but we do the job. If those of you who earn your primary income from doing business on this online auction site would like to be regarded as employees, eBay would be the second largest employer in the US after Wal-Mart. (Much the same is true in the UK.)

Given all this, no wonder that in 2006 we were all elected "Person of the Year" by *Time Magazine*. Man matters more than matter!

These days, individuals have also rid themselves from the geographical shackles of the past – 3is rule the world: individualists interacting internationally. The American Revolution of 1776 gave birth to the age of achievement – you got status from what you did, rather than the position you were born into. Chance was replaced by choice. The digitization and deregulation revolutions of the late 20th and early 21st centuries have opened up the ability for each and every one of us to internationalize our achievements. Now we all (possibly with the exception of those living in North Korea) belong to Gen C – Generation Choice.

The global stage is OURS. Enjoy the show. Then, make up your mind if the difference that you're going to make is red-hot positive, icy-cold negative, or if you're willing to settle for just being average and luke-warm. We all face the choice of +, 0 or –, now, every day. Because at the intensely and internationally competitive People's Party of the 21st century, you either lead the way or you'll be asked to leave. Adored or ignored. The choice is yours.

## Ruling in a world without rules

The world has changed. You have more power than ever before – potentially. And yet, you and your organization need to change. Now, you have to make the new rules.

Think back. In the not too distant past, it seemed as if life was pretty predictable – boring, perhaps, but at least foreseeable. The West was battling the East, GM, Ford and Chrysler were fighting to get their hands on the wallets of their American customers, and at Wimbledon Björn Borg always played John McEnroe. Some of us were rich – eternally. Others were poor – eternally. Before the age of plastic surgery with all its nips and tucks, certain people were beautiful, while others seemed to have been beaten with an ugly-stick – for life. You settled at the place where you were born. We knew who our friends and enemies were. Competitors had names that you could pronounce without twisting your tongue.

We were all brought up with the notion that the place where we worked today was also where we were supposed have a job tomorrow . . . and the day after tomorrow. Expectations were clear. Organizations were inhabited by thinkers and tinkerers. Some led and others followed. The future was given – almost written in tablets of stone. That was then. This is now – times during which it appears impossible to guess what's around the next corner – or even to know where the next corner is. Miss it, however, and in business you're off to the corporate coroner. Sadly or gladly, the future just isn't what it used to be. Certainty has been replaced by a genuine lack of control.

You rule – but in an era with few if any rules. In a lawless world, we should all expect the unexpected from the most unexpected. We were recently reminded that the author Mark Twain noted that the best swordsman in the world shouldn't fear the second-best. Rather, he should watch out for the one who knows little or nothing about fencing. Why? The ignorant person will probably come after him or her with moves and attacks that are much more difficult to anticipate.

Welcome to the world of *ignorant intelligence*. Nothing new really. Remember what happened to Christopher Columbus back in 1492. The man was, after all, on his way to India . . . Then, move some 500 years ahead and think of Iron Mike Tyson as he's staggering around trying to put his mouthpiece back after he's been knocked out by James "Buster" Douglas. Or, recall the minutes of footage from Michael Moore's *Fahrenheit 911* documentary of George W. Bush in Florida after he's been informed about the terrible twin towers tragedy.

## For whom the bell tolls

As we write, legendary companies like Ford and GM are hanging on the ropes. They're not alone. In May 2007, the New York-based private equity firm Cerbus acquired Chrysler for $7.4 billion – about 4.5 times more money than Google paid for the 67 YouTubers on top of the pizza parlor. Meanwhile, Toyota, a company that was seen as a joke by most Americans when it entered the US car-market 50 years ago with its first sales company and the Toyota Crown, now makes as much money as the rest of the global automotive industry combined. After the first quarter of 2007, Toyota also passed GM to become the largest corporation in the automotive industry. In terms of stock-market value, it surpassed Chrysler by almost 3000%. The car in front *is* a Toyota.

Vive la change! The leading mobile phone company in the world used to be a respectable manufacturer of rubber boots and toilet paper. Finnish corporation Nokia now controls more than one third of the market. In the meantime, the bell has almost tolled for Alexander Graham Bell's legacy – AT&T – which was broken up and then broke down. These days, all corporations are on the list of economically endangered species – always. Or, as Microsoft's Bill Gates once put it: "We are never more than 18 months away from failure."

Failure – or the threat of failure – is everywhere. It touches everything. Even the notion of a happy marriage is an endangered species. In many parts of the world, married couples are now a minority. Combining making a living with a good life is no walk in the park.

So, people ask us: what will our kids do when they grow up? Will Europe and the US stand a chance against well-educated and hard-hard-hard-working Chinese and Indians? How will Web 2.0 impact on our business? It sometimes seems as if the business world is governed by Zimbabwe's Robert Mugabe – you have no idea about what's going to happen next. Little wonder an increasing number of executives appear to be sleeping like babies – they wake up every two hours and cry.

The interesting thing is that many organizations (like most people) have a tendency to worry about the wrong things. A friend of ours, management guru Tom Peters, points out that GM worried about Ford and vice versa. People at IBM lost sleep over what Siemens and Fujitsu were up to. Sears was bothered by Kmart. Xerox was obsessed with Kodak and IBM. But it was bolts from the blue that broke them.

In discontinuous times, the past and the present aren't the fabulous kind of predictors of the future that they used to be. In fact, looking in the rear-view mirror will probably lead you in a direction that's completely wrong. History can be a lousy teacher for how to best prepare for the unlikely, unheard and the unseen. Read history, don't consign yourself to history.

# 3 In search of surprise

## Shift patterns

Ladies and Gentlemen, whether we like it or not, shifts happen!

Look around. As we were writing, in May 2007, Northern Ireland got a new power-sharing government headed by DUP leader Ian Paisley and Sinn Fein's Martin McGuiness. The two were so cozy together that newspapers labeled them the Chuckle Brothers (after a British children's TV slapstick act). To say Paisley and McGuiness aren't natural bedfellows is an under-statement in the extreme. It's akin to French footballer Zinedine Zidane calling his Italian nemesis Marco Materazzi to ask if he wants to join his family for vacation next summer!

More breaking news as we were writing: British business genius Lord Browne left BP after having lied in court about how he picked up a young Canadian male escort. (The lesson: If you're going to lie about such things and still keep your job, don't do it in court in front of a judge, but on TV in front of millions of viewers; be the president of a country, rather than a highly successful company; and go for a female intern instead of a male escort!)

Surprise, surprise. In 2006, the Nobel Peace Prize was awarded to a Bangladesh banker and economics professor – Muhammad Yunnus. The dismal science never seemed so worthwhile. Meanwhile, the most decorated movie at the 2006 Academy Awards was *Brokeback Mountain* with three Oscars. Directed by Chinese Ang Lee, it's a romantic Western about two homosexual cowboys. Just try to imagine that movie coming out of Hollywood some 20 or 25 years ago – starring John Wayne and Clint Eastwood!

More hard news: The global steel industry is now dominated by Indian companies! The owner of Mittal Steel, Laksmi Mittal, is the fifth richest person on our planet. And, super investor Warren Buffett gave $31 billion to the Bill and Melinda Gates Foundation. He also criticized the

US tax system for taxing him less than his secretary. Caring capitalism is apparently no longer an oxymoron. Great airplane food will be with us some time soon.

There's still more. Disney has opened up its first theme-park in Hong Kong. As one commentator put it: Mickey Mouse goes Mickey Mao! In 2005, IBM divested its entire PC-division to Chinese competitor Lenovo. Not that long ago, this seemed as likely as China off-shoring rice-farming to Finland!

Finally, the two most famous celebrity chefs are British. One is called the naked chef and the other one most men wanted to see naked!

## Every day is Christmas

Keep your eyes peeled. There are surprises at every turn. Surprise was kind of nice when you turned five. Your parents came into your room and you got to open presents. Of course, like you, we did not get the fancy stuff that parents buy their kids today – a teddy bear or a Barbie rather than a Playstation3 or an iPod, but it was still kind of neat. Oh boy, do things change.

Most sane people don't find it a very pleasant experience to be woken up at 6 o'clock Monday morning by a colleague who tells them that during the weekend there's been a big surprise at the factory or at one of their most important Chinese suppliers. Surprise, by definition, can be positive or negative – plus or minus.

Curiosity may have killed a cat or two, but it's usually when our own conservative way of thinking and behaving is messed up by the element of surprise that things start going to hell for the rest of us. So, whether you sleep like a baby or not, the time has come to re-connect with your inner-child. We all live, work, and have to do business in a _surprise society_. You and your colleagues face a business world of constant change, chaos and commotion – a world in which the unlikely has indeed become likely.

In recent years, what some people refer to as the ETBS – the *Expected Time Between Surprises* – has come down, and it has come down quite dramatically. Twenty-first century surprises come in a variety of shapes and forms. We're exposed to plenty of political and social surprise. Examples of cultural and economic surprise abound, not to mention what we experience in sports and science. It's increasingly difficult to figure out what will happen, when, how and who will initiate change. Therefore, leading change is no longer optional. To survive, mastering organizational change and re-energizing your troops is mandatory. As someone once put it; change is the price that we pay for survival.

# ETBS

EXPECTED TIME BETWEEN SURPRISES

How often were you and your company taken by surprise last week, last month and last year? What predictable surprises are brewing in your industry and organization right now? Do you have what it takes to anticipate and deal with them in a creative and constructive way? No matter what happened to you today, tomorrow is another day. Try to control the uncertainties of a surprise society and you'll go nuts. Surprise can neither be avoided nor controlled.

## To be surprised or . . .

People and organizations can relate to change in two very different ways. You may of course settle for constantly being surprised, spending the rest your business life like a punch-drunk boxer fighting the Mohammad Ali of your industry.

In our times of turmoil, this "become history rather than make history" approach largely equals crises management. You'll have to get involved in constant fire-fighting – trying to counter moves made by your competitors. Unfortunately, your job will be relegated to doing an infinite series of business autopsies without ever enjoying the kind of glory you would get on TV for revealing the identity of an arsonist or a serial killer.

Most people who fail to create the future have a propensity to be stability sadists, prophets of predictability and often have an almost perverted preference for what's eternal rather than that which is excellent. They thrive on exploiting current competitive advantages but constantly fail in experimenting for the future. These folks are destined to be eternally surprised – never to be the creators of positive change that astonishes the rest of us – neither customers nor colleagues or shareholders.

Those who do create the future – and these people are anything but average and normal – from Alexander the Great to Sir Bob Geldof – know that in order to succeed you must accept personal risk and be prepared to fail. Try translating that to reality in your own organization. How well would failure go down?

Think about it. Innovation boils down to experimentation. Experiments are risky – we can fail or succeed. A zero-failure rate can only be guaranteed if we stop all experimentation, but in today's economy that's also the surest way to fall behind.

We sometimes ask executives, how many of them made at least one semi-strategic mistake during the last 12 months. Hesitantly, between 5 and 10% of the participants raise their hands (interestingly, but not surprisingly, many more North Americans than Europeans or Asians do so). We don't worry about those people. But, we're deeply concerned about the rest. As a leader charged with the task of creating the future, how can you work for one year without making a single mistake and then hope to be the success-shocker of your industry? Are you spending too much time re-living the glory of the past and not enough on re-inventing for the future? Unfortunately, at most organizations, the fear of failure is as big as Jabba the Hut, while the passion for the prize of victory is as tiny as Master Yoda.

So, what are the implications for those who aspire to become masters of positive and disruptive change? Well, as an executive put it during a Tom Peters conference, to thrive under such circumstances, we must start punishing mediocre success and rewarding magnificent mistakes. What's merely mediocre can never be a surprise. Only that which is magnificent and truly spectacular can, at least potentially, provide you with a sustainable competitive edge, as an individual or a corporation. By definition, leaders of positive change must be CDOs – Chief Destruction Officers. They destroy to build and don't fear failure.

At your company, do you hand out Major Screw-Up of the Year (MSU) awards? In the army, we give medals – purple hearts and iron crosses – to those who have taken risks and been injured. Getting wounded is certainly not included in the job description of a soldier. It's a semi-strategic mistake.

Did you make at least one semi-strategic mistake last year? We hope you answered yes, because otherwise, there's a clear risk that you belong to the group of surprised rather than the surprise-bunch. Did you get a medal for it? Punish negative surprise and positive surprise won't happen. Success and failure are complementary. The man behind Dilbert, Scott Adams sums it all up: "Accept that some days you're the pigeon, and some days you're the statue."

## . . . be the surprise!

There's a different route than the one down the Boulevard of Broken Dreams that leads straight to Mount Stunned. It's deceptively simple. Don't play defense. Do something offensive. The only possible road to riches requires that you focus your attention, energy and efforts on being the surprise of your industry. The real leadership challenge of the new millennium is to become a constructive serial entrepreneur, a corporate activist, a driver of discontinuity, a re-energizing leader of positive change. Re-energized leadership is the electricity that powers all successful organizations. Without it, your people will remain in darkness.

And it's never too late to repent. Like George Foreman after "the rumble in the jungle", as you're lying there on the canvas staring at the pale African moon you may try to analyze why you didn't see it coming and then do something about it. George lay back and learned. He moved on and proved that it's never too late to lead change. At the tender age of 45, George made an unexpected come-back, and then made a fortune endorsing Salton grills (a gig originally offered to the legendary wrestler Hulk Hogan). Lean, mean and still grilling.

Surprise translates into lucrative business. The Holy Grail of economic theory and practice is called a "temporary monopoly". This concept was coined almost a century ago by legendary Austrian economist Joseph Schumpeter – a man who claimed that as a young man he aspired to be the best man in Vienna at three things: a lover, a horseman, and an economist. Schumpy died confessing that much to his regret he had only managed to succeed in two of his pursuits of happiness but would never say which. (Google an image of the man for a hint . . .)

To make ridiculous amounts of money, for a short moment in time and/or in space, individuals, corporations and regions must offer us something that's absolutely unique – stuff that we've never seen or heard or felt or smelt or tasted before. In business life, as in life in general, success boils down to avoiding competition while simultaneously capturing demand. Both requirements are equally important. A man who finds himself in lesbian club may think he has limited competition, but is sooner or later destined to realize that there's no demand.

The brightest shining stars in business, sports, music and art, and especially those that continue to shine on like crazy diamonds, are always *different* rather than merely better. Focus on being better and you're basically placing your bets on the stupidity of your competitors. As tempting as this procedure may seem, it's usually a terribly silly strategy to pursue. Some of your existing competitors may be managed by morons, but don't forget that most of your future competitors are probably still unborn. Bet on their idiocy at your own peril. We wager that at least some of them will surprise you!

Behind all temporary monopolies, from Fosbury's flop to Microsoft's Vista, we always find an idea that surprises competition and customers – the former group in a negative way and the latter in a more positive manner. Leaders capable of re-energizing create and translate such ideas into action – ideas that are difficult to imitate – and deliver unique value in an inimitable way. They make change happen. These people also excel at creating conditions enabling the rest of the organization to become more prone to produce surprise. They know that while you build competitiveness cumulatively, it can disappear instantly. Twenty-first century leadership requires that re-energizing executives accept overall responsibility for the WOW-element – the surprise-factor!

The distinctive difference that's necessary for profits to occur may of course be implemented in various ways, on different levels, including the following:

- The *purpose* of the organization may be unique, as expressed through its vision or mission – the dream. Some organizations just have a different calling. Médicins sans Frontières, for example, is about more than money. The Red Cross exists to "help the most needed". Merely focusing on creating shareholder value is trivial. Most of your competitors will not focus their efforts on destroying shareholder value – at least not on purpose.
- Other firms focus on having a unique *portfolio* of products and services, emphasizing the scope or ability to deliver integrated systems. Swedish telecommunications star Ericsson is the world-leader in mobile systems, based on its integration capabilities.
- Some companies live off a *hit product* or service, or a series thereof. MacIntosh + iMac + iPod + iMusic + iPhone (?) = Apple. Surf's up. Let's find the next big wave.
- Many successful contemporary corporations have configured their *processes* into unique and hyper-efficient business models. Just look at Dell Computers or British retail wonder Tesco.

- Finally, there are those organizations, like management consultants McKinsey or the media house St Luke's, that rely heavily on the exceptional talent of their *people*.

Truly excellent enterprises (including some of those mentioned above), usually base their competitiveness on implementing rarity at much more than one level. What about your organization – in what ways, are you distinctly different, today and tomorrow? Questions abound. How difficult would it be for someone to imitate what you currently base the competitiveness of your corporation on? Who's responsible for making sure that you remain competitive? Unless you have a point of view about the future today, tomorrow may not happen.

Re-energized leadership is about making a positive difference in these dimensions so that value is constantly created for your customers, shareholders, the organization, your employees and yourself. Pro-active rather than re-active leadership makes a positive difference. To get started, take an hour or so to think about the future of your corporation or team, using the grid below. Tomorrow, gather your team and start envisioning what's next.

| Level of implementation | Current differentiation | Future opportunity | Responsibility |
|---|---|---|---|
| 1. *Purpose* | | | |
| 2. *Portfolio* | | | |
| 3. *Products & Services* | | | |
| 4. *Processes* | | | |
| 5. *People* | | | |

.

# The energy of excellence

**4**

## In search of speed

A well-known executive once said that in the future there will be two types of companies; the quick and the dead! Like it or not, history has proven this correct. Either we're fast or we'll be forgotten. This is a speed or pack up business world! To provide the surprise and make sure that you're the first one to create the future, your corporation will need momentum. If you paid attention at school you're probably familiar with the fact that in physics velocity is a function of mass and energy – the lower the mass and the greater the energy the faster an object moves.

$$V=f(M,E)$$

There's a business translation of the equation. In recent years, most companies, at least in the West, have been obsessed with processes focused on de-massification. Now, in all likelihood you're not familiar with de-massification, but you've probably heard of downsizing and rightsizing, out-sourcing and off-shoring. Same thing – big thing. Founded some 25 years ago, Indian IT consulting and service specialist Infosys pioneered strategic O-O – "outsource-offshoring". Today, the firm has 75 000+ employees and annual revenues recently crossed the $2 billion mark.

In an effort to create the asset-light organization that competes on its intellectual capital (IC), most corporations in the West have converted to the de-massification religion. Right now, just about everything, bar the core competences of the firm, are under pressure from the outside – the not so invisible hand(s) of the mighty market. Contemporary companies seek to become ever fast*er*, smart*er*, cheap*er* and bett*er*. The main ingredients of the dominant business recipe of the past decade have therefore been spelt *re*-engineering, *re*-aligning, *re*-structuring and *re*-organizing. Most leaders of major corporations prefer to *re* rather than err.

The business case for de-massifying is easily made. Deregulation, digitization and globalization have taken us on a journey from a world of locally isolated information deserts into an internationally integrated information jungle where markets rule and reign. Things that you once had to build in-house can now be bought from someone else, somewhere else. So, we do. People do it with their laundry, gardens and childcare. Governments do it with customer relationship management, IT infrastructure and applications. Corporations do it with just about everything.

Anything can be outsourced – the hard stuff as well as the soft. Around 31% of the total electronics market is now globally outsourced. Headquartered in Singapore, Flextronics helps customers design, build, ship, and service electronics products through a network of facilities in over 30 countries and five continents. In your home, you almost certainly have lots of stuff that has been touched by people from this firm. You just don't know about it.

Moreover, people that you once had to employ can now work for you but be engaged by someone else, somewhere else. Manpower, one of the world leaders in the employment services industry, has a worldwide network of 4400 offices in 73 countries and annually serves 400 000 customers. It has a staff of some 30 000 people and provides employment opportunities to an astonishing 4.4 million associates per year. That's more people than the population of a decent sized country such as Ireland.

## Seduced by slim fast diets

Ditching bulk is all-alluring. The short-term cost-savings of such arrangements are easily calculated, while any negative effects on the long-term competitiveness of the firm – in the form of damaged tacit knowledge, disconnected relationships or diminishing employee engagement – are more remote in time, surrounded by more ambiguity and often quite difficult to measure.

Since man is fundamentally a quick-fix, uncertainty-reducing animal, the seductive power of the shrink-to-greatness business-model approach has proved enormous. Unfortunately, the starving corporation rarely ends up as the new Kate Moss of their industry.

There are many examples of companies that have dumped activities and components, people and processes that management believed could no longer provide them with a competitive edge. Often, the only thing that these "state-of-the-art" organizations are left to compete with is the knowledge which is located in the minds of a few key employees.

No religion can guarantee entrance to Nirvana. Similarly, no management theory is perfect. De-massification comes with a number of caveats:

- Sustainable competitive advantages can't be based on outsourcing. As soon there's a well-functioning market for something, also your competitors potentially have access to it. Farming out to the best is consequently a bit like having access to a really nice toilet back at the office – necessary but not sufficient for succeeding in your pursuit of competitiveness. You may of course combine things bought from someone else in an innovative way, but don't expect stand-alone suppliers to provide you with a competitive advantage, even if they are called SAP or Accenture. Consider this. Taiwanese electronic equipment manufacturer Hon Hai makes close to half of all the mobile phones in the world – almost all of them for other brands. Do you think they provide the other players with any sustainable competitive advantages? Thought not.
- Articulate knowledge – that which we can write down with a pen on a piece of paper and in an e-mail (or a business book) with the help of a computer or communicate orally – is increasingly becoming a commodity. Competence producing organizations are now more numerous, geographically dispersed and uniform than ever before. Across the face of planet earth, standardized MBAs and MScs abound. The best engineering and medical schools aren't in the US or Europe, but in India. A good degree is no longer a vaccine against the Asian business flu. You're not alone. We're not alone.
- Numerous studies show that in today's non-linear economy, long-term success must be based on innovation rather than optimization. Maximizing knowledge creation, rather than minimizing transaction costs, is the new road to riches. Again, we need to separate what's merely necessary from that which is also sufficient for the creation of surprise and success, change and competitiveness.
- When corporations get rid of mass, this procedure often causes energy leakage and employee engagement deteriorates with consequent declining performance. We may laugh at the Dilbert cartoon that goes;

- Knock, knock.
- Who's there?
- Not you anymore!

Yet, anyone who has ever worked in an organization where the downsizing demon has run havoc knows what this business version of Tobe Hooper's *Texas Chainsaw Massacre* does to the spirit of people, even those still around. Genius rarely performs well when you put a gun to its head. Why be creative and do great deeds for your organization today, when tomorrow you may be dead?

## Beyond nerdville

For modern companies, doing the de-massification gig has become a required, but no longer satisfactory, condition for the creation of a sustainable competitive edge. Yet, at the same time, many organizations have by and large neglected the other variable of the function – energy. And this is critical, because within the energy dimension of the corporation we find two other types of capital that are absolutely critical to the future competitiveness of any organization: psychological and social capital (PC and SC).

When you can no longer base any sustainable competitive advantages on superior access to physical or financial capital, it's instead your ability to tap into the other sources of wealth creation – IC, PC and SC – that determines your level of success. In our experience, these three currencies of competitiveness are related to one another in a multiplicative rather than an additive way. Even a small drop in any type of capital may cause tremendously negative effects on your organization's ability to be a positive surprise.

# ICxPCxSC

As we shall see, in a world of economic Darwinism, only firms that offer something that's either as fit as the great white shark or as sexy as a peacock's tail stand a genuine chance of survival. Yet, it doesn't take a genius to conclude that Dell has been really fit and Apple insanely sexy, or that Singapore Airlines or Malaysian Airways base their competitiveness on something quite different from the likes of low-cost airlines Ryan Air or South West Airlines. We've so far, however, not been able to come up with a comprehensive theory for how to organize and lead a corporation that keeps on spawning new products and services that continue to astonish and addict customers.

We believe that the first clue to understanding the answer to this everlasting question rests with considering not only the intellectual challenges, but also those related to the psychological and social capital of people and organizations. Entrepreneurial leaders who re-energize their organizations are similar to great gardeners. They know that while you make money on the fruits of the trees you grow, over time, you cultivate these trees from the roots up. And exactly here, at the level of the roots of the corporation, is where we find the future potential of an organization – ICxPCxSC.

To thrive, the next challenge that contemporary leaders of business face is therefore the one of re-energizing the corporation – to accept responsibility for creating a better future. The 1990s gave us a competence-based view of the firm. Now, the time has come to move on and profit also from psychology- and sociology-based perspectives that help executives boost employee engagement and the energy level of the enterprise.

## Blessed synchronicity

Time and time again, we'll return to how leaders who excel at re-energizing their corporations, divisions, business areas, teams or units transform them into simultaneous systems of synchronized fantasy, feelings and faith. They know that future success requires a combination of know-how, can-do and know-who. Merely getting one or two out of these processes right will no longer do the trick.

By embracing a positive and innovative leadership style based on your own strengths, you can thrive in a topsy-turvy economy. Remember IBM, Man U, Al Gore and Madonna. In fact, surprise opens up as many new potential breaks and prospects as threats or challenges. Leaders capable of re-energizing their organizations excel at turning surprises into superior opportunities. Attitude is everything.

A number of pundits now claim that the proper response to a shrinking ETBS is for companies to install an EWS – Early Warning System. We beg to differ. Based on our experience, instead of installing early warning systems, progressive leaders of positive change operate with an 24/7 EOS – Early Opportunity System. They realize that stability will not get you anywhere. Disruptivity, on the other hand, always gets you somewhere. Re-energizing leaders envision, engage and execute for excellence!

# 5   Energizing leadership

## The leadership tour

People often ask us; isn't it more difficult to be a great leader today than it has ever been before? The short answer is; NO! Let's give you an example. When J. Sigfried Edström took over the helm at ASEA, the Swedish company that would later form one part of ABB, in the early 20th century, he decided to visit all the group subsidiaries to get a grip on the entire corporate body. The trip, mostly by boat and train, took several months!

Surprise isn't an entirely new phenomenon. Today, Cisco's John Chambers boasts that he can close the books of this multi-billion dollar company any minute of any day of the week. No, it's not more difficult to lead, but the current challenges are quite different from those of the past.

## Into the great wide open

The very nature of the challenge facing leaders is changing. Once upon a time, a newly appointed manager inherited a business recipe from his or her predecessor and was given the task of maximizing the corporate benefits of this everlasting formula. No more! The expiration date of everything from product and service life cycles to systems and procedures are changing at a pace that has made innovation a necessity – possibly, some may see it as an evil one, but it's still a fact of business life. Erase the words eternal, given, predictable and standard from your vocabulary. While you're at it, don't forget to replace stability with surprise. The future is a much more moveable feast than ever before.

If your business life is anything like the ones of executives who we've been working with over the last few years, the socio-economic landscape that you need to make sense of (because you can't control it – so give up that idea at once) and sense-make also to others (possibly your most important task) is at times both plagued by enormous levels of uncertainty caused by all the surprises and almost ungraspable in scope. Welcome to the new instant multi-reality, multi-technology, multi-national, multi-functional, multi-institutional world that you must organize and lead at the speed of light.

To succeed in envisioning the future, not only will you have to utilize the competence of yourself and those around you. As a leader, you'll also be held accountable for explaining the context so that the challenges that your team should be working on, and which when properly executed will provide you with a temporary monopoly, are clearly understood by everyone else. If you're a good leader, you're probably intelligent as hell. Don't expect everyone else to get it, just because you get it. Get it?

## The disobedient masses

There's more. This is our experience. What about yours? As you approach your team to tell people what needs to be done, what used to be the unthinkable often happens. Your colleagues (or for the unenlightened – subordinates) no longer snap to attention just because you happen to be their boss. You can't tell them what to do.

Let's face it. There's no longer that much tolerance for a command and control style of leading. Recent changes in society have awakened within many of the minds of today's workforce the need to know **why** they are asked to do things – high-maintenance but also high-performance. They also want, or for some it's more of a basic need, to find that their personal values are aligned with what they are being asked to do by their employer. Scandals like World Com, Enron and Shell have made unquestioning loyalty a thing of the corporate past. No one likes to think that they have invested their personal energy into an organization that demands obedience and blind followers. Instead, people with the freedom of choice respond extremely well to socially responsible companies.

Smart people are no Nikes – they just won't do it. So, once you have a point of view or an idea about what tomorrow could and should be like, you simply can't start implementing. Instead, the in-house marketing and sales process commences. Without internal buy-in, there will never be external buy-in, and without that there will never be any cash coming in your way.

You may also have noticed that especially the young and super-sharp ones in your talent pool have a really hard time dealing with formal authority. In fact, you probably shouldn't tell them what to do and how to do it – if you're any good at recruiting top-talent they ought to be smarter than you (at least in their particular area of expertise). Once you have talent inside, to truly profit from your investment in IC, you have to use your creativity to figure out how to maximize the return on competence as well as how to retain and develop them.

As if all that wasn't enough, some of these people may even speak a different language and come from a culture that in many respects is distinctly different from the one that you were brought up in. A few of them will probably not even be under your jurisdiction as they formally work for someone else – Cognizant, Manpower, or Infosys. Perhaps several of them are already located in another country. Tomorrow, trust us, they almost certainly will be.

Most of these gold-collar workers have at least two things in common. No. 1, truce or not, many of them subscribe to the old Marxist idea that we, the people, now control the most critical resources of our economy – our own minds – though individually rather than collectively.

No. 2, most of these folks just don't work out of moral obligations. It would be easy to proclaim them disloyal. We beg to differ. That would mean greatly misreading what drives this group of people. The level of loyalty that we find in a society tends to be reasonably constant, but it's shifting. Decades and centuries ago, loyalty used to be imposed on us by kings and queens, czars and emperors, generals and dictators, popes or priests. Then it became self-imposed. Of course, peer-pressure, traditional norms and values emphasizing the role of work, collectivism and obedience still rule the lives of many people. For many, normality is still the norm and something to strive for. But for true talent, loyalty is self-directed.

Leadership by merely telling will not get you anywhere. Leadership by talking – discussing, debating, dialoguing, deliberating or conversing, chatting, consulting . . . call it whatever you want – is mandatory if you want to go for meritocracy rather than mediocrity. You have to earn trust by oozing confidence. It's really 360 degree confidence we're talking about. You must be confident in yourself and them. Likewise, they have to be confident in themselves and you. Trust is a give and take process.

Without this ability to engage people – transforming time and energy invested in individual relationships into an informal contract which says, "Yes, I will die 4U" (the Prince-test of leadership) – you're nothing and no matter the speed of your intellect you'll never be able to get past Nowhereville! Recall Martin Luther King Jr.'s observation: "If a man hasn't discovered something that he will die for, he isn't fit to live."

## Short and sweet

When the time has come for you and your team to deliver on your promises, the impact of an ever more short-sighted stock-market is yet another thing to consider. Millions of anonymous capitalists are sitting in front of their computer screens in their shorts and a t-shirt, sipping a coke trying not to go broke. Young MBAs in pin-stripe suits from some investment fund in another country that owns 5% of your company keep on bothering you. These people all have one thing in common. They are in it for the quick buck – their own or someone else's. The consequences are crystal clear: Deliver exceptional output – or you become an output. How you execute the strategy may not be everything, but it still matters a great deal.

Competitive pressure is reaching boiling-point. Most industries – from bulk chemicals to PCs – are characterized by over-capacity. The number one business impact of all IT-investments has been increased productivity. Are you familiar with Demi Moore's Law? It was covered in a *Harvard Business Review* article and states that IT-related productivity gains increase at half the pace of the more familiar Moore's Law – so every 36 to 48 months we should expect these to double. While this principle has a positive impact on the level of a single firm, the industry implications are more problematic. When everyone is racing for the productivity frontier, using the same software from Microsoft, Oracle and SAP and the same hardware from Dell, Lenovo and HP Compaq, don't be surprised that the inevitable end-result is over-capacity. And when supply is greater than demand prices and profits come down.

From all this follows that there's a closing window of opportunity with increased calls for rapid execution and greater personal risks if you fail. Be courageous or you'll be carried out. Total, global, cut-throat, competence-based competition probably also implies that your competitors, the born and the unborn – external as well as internal – will be trying to rob you of your best people. Given that talent is a scarce resource, at times, you'll have to deal with a severe capacity shortage. Perhaps you already do? Since knowledge is perishable – it comes with a best before date – as a leader set on re-energizing, you'll also have to assume responsibility for making sure that the capabilities of you and your team are up-to-date.

Are you thirsty for more challenges? Yet, we promise that leading talent through change isn't like herding cats. It can be done. You can do it!

## 6 Killed by management

## Start with failure

In practice, re-energizing an entire corporation or even a small team is easier said than done. But, it can be done, as witnessed by many of the leaders who we've coached. The first big challenge to confront is the fact that, just like your personal life, your business life must be lived forward, but is best understood backward. The process of becoming a successful leader, capable of re-energizing and making change happen, begins with understanding the true nature of failure. Only by looking death straight in the face, can we begin to understand how to avoid entering the decline sequence of denial, deterioration and death that got to the ancient Greeks, Simple Minds and DEC.

In all likelihood, you're set on leading an organization, a team, or whatever that's at least an above average performer. Doesn't beating mediocrity sound very aspirational and inspirational? Well, keep in mind that while the Roman Empire may not be around, Rome wasn't built in a day. So let's start with a modest proposal (after all, one of us is Swedish): Our initial aim is to learn how to beat the market.

## Losing your religion

To begin with, take a few seconds to reflect. What do you think are the chances of running or working for a company that consistently performs better than the index, above average? We're not talking about being featured on the cover of *Fortune* or *Time* like the guys from Google or becoming the next Steve Jobs, interviewed live by Larry King on CNN. We're just looking at the odds of a corporation being more than merely ordinary.

To find the answer to this question we need to travel in both time and space. Let's go back to 1917, take a trip to the US and look at the Forbes 100 companies – the 100 largest and finest companies the United States of America could offer back then.

Let's follow these corporations for 70 years up to 1987. Over that period, how many of them do you think managed to beat the index, the market – 50, 25, 10? Surprise! Research shows that the answer is two! Again, take some time to reflect. Which firms do you think we're looking at? Well, it turns out that General Electric and Eastman Kodak were the only corporations out of these 100 firms that ended up on the list of above average performers. By 1987, an astonishing 61 corporations of the Forbes class of 1917 were no longer around, and of the remaining 39 survivors, 18 significantly underperformed the market.

If we follow these companies for another 10 years, we're left with only one corporation – GE. Eastman Kodak experienced some Japanese "surprise!" during the late eighties and nineties. Perhaps they too began to worry about the wrong enemy? So (and this you shouldn't really include in a business bestseller), over time, it seems, the chances of beating mediocrity appear to be about 1%! No Dr. Feelgood here.

Now, you may object, and in all probability rightly so, that in a time of fleeting employee (and employer) loyalty and constant corporate career-hopping, few of us will spend 80 years in the same corporate trenches (though with the current advances in medicine combined with pension insecurities we wouldn't rule that out). Or, you could argue that you're not in the apparently ill-fated position to be the head of a big corporation like Ford or Chrysler.

Why don't we then look at a different sample – Standard & Poor's 500. More companies here, not only the mega-big behemoths – none of them are midgets, however. Let's look at their performance between 1957 and 1997. The results, we promise you, look a whole lot better. Studies suggest that it's not only a meager 1% that manages to beat the market – statistically speaking it's much more than that; some 2.4%! The survival rate is also up to 74%.

This isn't solely a Western phenomenon. In life-time employment oriented South Korea only seven of the top 100 companies in 1955 were on the list in 2004. In fact, the crisis in 1997 destroyed half of the country's 30 largest conglomerates.

So, what went so terribly wrong? Why do most once great organizations end up as extinct as the Dodo? What factors explain the difficulties in consistently out-performing the market? Because if you were to expect any companies to make it, the Forbes 100 and S&P 500 firms would all belong to the group of the usual suspects. No other corporations had access to that kind of money, larger buildings, more sophisticated machinery and greater people. But, still almost all of them came to realize as composer Irving Berlin once noted: "The toughest thing about success is that you've got to keep on being a success."

When we bring up these issues with executives, most are quiet for about half a minute or so. Then, they tend to say things like, "success breeds complacency" or "size brings about bureaucracy". The real problem is that they are exceptionally reluctant to include the implied antidotal slogans of "securing our future with fast, furious failures" or "domination by designing for decline" in their own mission statements.

## Deviance destruction

Over the last century, hoards of business school professors and consultants have worked really hard to invent a concept to remedy the situation – a cure against all known ills in business. We're of course thinking about a well known term to all of you; it begins with man- and ends with -agement – **management**. If we could only manage our organization in a more professional way than the others we should end up as the 1% company. Accordingly, the traditional recipe for getting a company back on track has been the application of more management and more control to show that you're in command.

Next big question: what *is* management? We suspect that in all probability you're a manager. Hence, what you do must be management. So, what do you do during an ordinary (!) day at the office?

*Arrivecheckemailmeetingcoffeeanothermeetingphone callslunchgototoiletyetanothermeetingmorecoffeesendemails writeprogressreporttoiletetcgohomeatsix!*

Does this standard sequence sound familiar? Over the years, management has been given great many definitions – from the early writing of pioneers like Henri Fayol and Chester Bernard to later denizens such as Peter Drucker and Gary Hamel. Historically, managers planned, organized, supervised and coordinated. And since they could not trust the poor bastards they were in charge of managers were also supposed to control that these people actually did what they were told to do.

We prefer a different definition, however – slightly more abstract perhaps, but nevertheless based on the practical application of the concept. During the 20th century, management was largely defined as the art of assuring organizational order. To achieve this objective, executives were supposed to destroy deviance – primarily negative deviance, but if a couple of positive deviants were killed in the process that was a sacrifice which most companies were willing to make in the name of professional management.

- We hunted down and killed diversity by creating Amish-like organizations where everyone looked the same and people betted on the chance that they could freeze time by planning the future. One of us recently did a conference with one of the world's most admired corporations. No expenses spared. During the event, company executives bashfully admitted that during the corporation's first global meeting not a single woman attended. The men were lodged in so-called two-men tents – like GI Joe's – and had loads of fun, though not in the tents management assured the audience. The first woman to attend one of these meetings did so in 1956 (we're not totally sure if she had loads of fun). This, of course, was a few years ago and things have improved. But, at the senior levels, most organizations are still homo-focused, uni-color, and obsessed with being in command.
- We stamped out standard-deviation and eliminated "waste" by applying management techniques such as TQM, BPR and ISO 9000, 9001, 9002, 9003 or ninethousandwhatsoever with zealous discipline. It's interesting to note that a modern management method like Six Sigma literally stands for 99.99967% zero-deviance. Ironically, in a surprise society, models like these, with a patented emphasis on perfecting the known, sometimes inspire executives to do things that aren't roughly right but **exactly** wrong.
- We paid homage to homogeneity by keeping all strategic functions at one location, in one building where most important decisions were taken by "the man" in the corner office on the top floor. At times, this was the case even in the 1% company General Electric. There's an old GE story about how whenever the CEO asked for a cup of coffee, an employee went out and tried to buy Brazil. Also remember that the term bureaucracy does indeed stem from the French word

*bureau,* and in Max Weber's case the German *das buro* meaning office – the physical manifestation of the 20th century corporation.

Like the members of most conservative groups in the 20th century – from the Soviet Kremlin, prior to the entrance of Gorby, to many a corporate boardroom (or perhaps bored room is a more accurate description) – huge swathes of so called professional managers fought hard to keep the market forces of change and disruption outside their organizations. We buffered by integrating backward and forward. Coordination was based on centralized planning and decision-making. The principles applied were similar to those still used on Cuba and in North Korea. Examples of organizations relying on mutual adjustment between units within a dispersed corporate system of differentiated intelligence where you thrive on realizing that you're always dependent on someone else – perhaps even customers – (and increasingly this someone is located somewhere else, perhaps even institutionally), were rare. But in the US there was at least one exception – GE under Jack Welch.

## Mean averages

Until recently, management was focused on turning all things and most beings into standards and averages – identical parts that would be easily replaceable in a gigantic operating apparatus. How do you create sameness? Short answer; eliminate individual negative deviance. We turned our attention to the weaknesses of people and started to work on those. Our entire society, including most corporations, was obsessed with turning minuses into zeros – super-zeros, but still zeros. The fixation on weaknesses came at the expense of us developing the capability to grow our strengths.

Think about it. Almost from cradle to grave, we and our fellow citizens have been obsessed with curing illnesses rather than trying to practice preemptive medicine.

- It started at school. If you were really bad at math, you got extra help. Obviously, this was (and still is) laudable. While you would never get a Nobel Prize, it saved you from complete ignorance. But, what about the alternative use of the resources? Those who were fantastic had to cope on their own.
- When you get your first job, you're shipped off to HR for a mandatory gap-analysis. They may tell you that although your technical skills are brilliant, you're not that much of a sales person are you? Don't worry. They can always send you to this amazing training program. You will of course not return as a fantastic salesperson, but they do guarantee turning you into a super-zero kind of salesperson.
- Many managers still spend 80% of their time and attention on the 20% of the businesses, products or people that are the worst performers – the M&M's of business – Mega-Minuses. What would happen if we did the reverse?
- Before getting your first divorce you go to family therapy or marriage counseling. The shrink concludes that you're not this super-cuddly kind of person but promises that five years on the couch will at least transform you into a super-zero kind of husband or wife.

Or imagine that it's time for Albert Einstein's annual performance review at Super-zero Inc. What would you tell him? Buy a new suit and cut your hair? Get rid of that silly mustache and for God's sake stop being such an annoyance during our meetings?

In a world full of "simple" super-zero kind of people it appeared natural to build super-complex organizations. We moved from functional to divisional or multidivisional and then over to matrixes. Instead of organizing the firm as a brain, we betted on the wisdom of a few executives who would act as the brain of the firm. Brain-based organizational design implies that the totality is reflected in the parts through a shared understanding of the corporation's context and challenges, mission, vision and values. In this latter more holographic corporation, the entire organization can be recreated from any element – unit or person.

## The pursuit of plus

Today, we all know that peak performance must be based on our plusses – individual and corporate. Or as Peter Drucker put it: "A person can perform only from strengths. One can't build performance on weaknesses, let alone on something one can't do at all." If you're born tone-deaf, not even 350 years of practice will turn you into the next Luciano Pavarotti. Or, if you, like one of us, happened to be born with his left foot on his right leg, no amount of training will land you a contract with Italian football-club Inter Milan. Positive surprise is produced not by super-zeros but by super-heroes – those who learn to grow their plusses and leverage their strengths. The new leadership paradigm for 21st century corporations must therefore be preemptive instead of curative.

Never forget that we're all born with the potential to become a super-hero. "Every child is an artist. The problem is how to remain an artist once we grow up," said Picasso. Just like we have different blood types, there are different talent types. If we can only become really skilled at playing the cards in the hand that we were dealt, and help people around us to play their plusses, positive surprise will happen. Each and every person on our planet is a container of the potential for positive deviance. Our advice is simple; pursue your plusses.

In a world of increasing freedom of choice, the ability to know what you're really good at is one of the most important ones to possess. If you don't have a clue about your own strengths, begin by asking a few of your colleagues to write down a couple of instances when you've added significant value. Also remember that for real life supermen and women there's not any kryptonite that obliterates the power of individual creativity.

## Calculating business

As ludicrous as all the old-fashioned management procedures may seem (basking under the bright light of hindsight most things do), there were two different rationales behind this apparent madness – a psychological and an economic motive to destroy deviance. Most people prefer familiarity over novelty. Given a choice, your typical white, male executives age 55, will prefer to hire a White Anglo-Saxon Protestant (WASP) guy with a degree from his old alma mater Harvard, rather than a young, tongue-pierced woman with an exam from an unknown virtual business school.

As for the economic motive, back then, we guess, people on average were no more stupid than we are today. But, they did approach work with a different hypothesis. During the greater part of the 20th century, the name of the business game was spelt: efficiency. Executives were set with the task of perfecting the known. Long-range planning, economies of scale and scope, learning curves and productivity dominated the strategic thinking.

Here's the problem. While the variation extermination approach that management has been based on, so far, ensured that the corporation was rarely inefficient, the negative side effect was that in the face of radical and revolutionary change the organization almost by definition became irrelevant. Swedish firm Facit used to be the world leader in mechanical calculators. The company was well-managed and super efficient. In 1970, Facit was the Polar star of the Swedish business community, with 14 000 employees and subsidiaries in 100+ countries. In 1971, Japanese-made electronic calculators hit the market and Facit went out of business virtually over-night with its obsolete products. Not even Prussian-style efficiency helps when you're no longer relevant.

The principle is universal. Look no further than yourself. Imagine that you're at a bar or a club. It's Saturday evening. Your mission, if you chose to accept it, is to pick up someone. You're fresh out of the shower and smartly dressed. All your pick-up lines have been nicely rehearsed. You approach your "customer" and go to work. Now, imagine the following two responses;

- Alt 1. Sorry, but you're not very efficient are you . . .
- Alt 2. Sorry, but I find you completely irrelevant!

Although we guess none of the answers are exactly what you hoped for, alternative one at least provides you with an opportunity to practice and work innovatively on the tactics and come back. The second response is an invitation to go home and spend the rest of the evening watching *Saturday Night Live*.

Take our advice. Choose relevance over efficiency.

# 7 From great to grave

## Dial M for dilemmas

In *The Innovators Dilemma,* Harvard Business School's Clayton M. Christensen studied companies that once dominated their industries and then fell from the pedestal – great to grave corporations; a road that apparently is more traveled than the one that takes you from good to great. After years and years of research and teaching at the most prestigious business school in the world – the Taj Mahal of hyper-modern management – this was his key conclusion: "Good management was the most powerful reason they failed to stay atop their industries." Sometimes, it seems, the cure can actually be worse than the disease.

Most management models still only tell us how to become a little bit better at that which we're already pretty darn good at. The re-engineering frenzy, for instance, is all about boosting efficiency within an existing frame. Now, juxtapose this obsession with repetition rather than renewal with Einstein's definition of insanity: doing the same thing over and over again and expecting different results. It's no big secret that ensuring future competitiveness is dependent on us departing from the route well-trodden.

Creatures less intelligent than your average middle manager, like ants, for instance, are programmed to randomly depart from the path in order to find new food or building materials, not to over-exploit a particular area. The problem is that management, as we've defined it and applied the concept, is anti-evolutionary and pro-permanence. This also means that management often works against long-term peak performance.

Imagine that, if, after the first day of creation, God had taken a break to spend some time at business school to attend Management 101. (OK, as far as we know God did not create any well-known business schools during day one of Genesis, but as noted by British comedian Ricky Gervais we're talking about a guy who allegedly **created** light – it's not like it was there before – so let's assume that he could have put up a little business school – IKEA style – if there had been a need for it.) Consider the consequences. Adam and Eve wouldn't be around. Ditto you. By the way, neither would apples nor talking snakes (that later turned out not to be very competitive and joined 39 of the companies in the Forbes 100 class of 1917), but it would be dark as hell or so bright you had to wear shades.

We pay tribute to Clayton M. – the Salman Rushdie of the management profession – and his "Satanic Verses". The *uberguru* of disruptive business practices, Tom Peters, even goes as far as to argue that the main reason why GE ended up as the 1% corporation was exactly because it's (was?) – by FAAAAAAR according to Tom (not a man who will be remembered for his temperance) – the most disorganized of all the large North American multinationals. But hold your horses. Tom does say disorganized, not anarchical. As little as command and control will boost competitiveness will utter chaos and constant change lead to profitable growth. No matter how creative you are in your approach to running a corporation, to be able to think out of the box, you do need a box. Remember the new business principles from earlier: People + Purpose + Platform + Participation + Passion. This is a theme we'll return to.

## Eenie, meenie, miney, moe

So, we tried more management and it did not work. Then, what did we do? Who was to blame for all failures? Short answer; you guys – managers, of course! Paradoxically, this led to a situation in which people both started to admire them and then fire them – especially senior executives – to an extent that the world had never ever witnessed before. In the year 1980, the cover of *Fortune* featured one CEO. Twenty years later, the equivalent number was 19. During this period, the average expected lifetime of a chief executive officer also shrunk considerably. Research indicates that approximately 40% of new chief executives fail in their first 18 months. If you're in that position, when you think about your future, don't think the *Rolling Stones* – think *Pussycat Dolls*.

And if firing your managers doesn't yield results, what's next? If either the board or the top-management team begins to fear that you're heading for Never-Never-land, who do you think they are you going to call? No, it's not the Ghost Busters – but consultants. If your corporation can afford it, they may even call in McKinsey, the most royal of all corporate comforters – the best of the best. Out of the world's 200 largest companies, how many do you think work with this consulting firm? No, it's not all of them. We have to consider the fact that in this industry we find also the likes of BCG, Accenture, Roland Berger, etc, and McKinsey did get some bad press after the Enron-scandal. No, studies suggest that a mere 147 of the world's 200 largest organizations seek the advice of McKinsey. In financial services were looking at 80 of the top 120 firms and a stunning 9 out of the top 11 chemical companies.

So, apparently almost 75% of the greatest corporations in the world go to one firm. Apparently, they are hoping that this company and its consultants will provide them with unique . . . sustainable . . . long-term . . . competitive advantages. Good luck!

No wonder that one of us decided to call one of his previous books *Karaoke Capitalism*. You may not know this – for some odd reason, very few people admit to frequenting Karaoke Bars – but your friends can probably tell you that at the Karaoke bar you find a copy of a copy of a copy. Hardly surprising, in the era of global hyper-competition – think BRIC: Brazil, Russia, China and India – there's extremely limited pay-back in play-back. As Andrew Carnegie put it: "The first one gets the oyster while the second one gets the shell." With a considerable number of business schools becoming globally standardized and every-one doing bench-marking and sharing best-practices, we've reached the end of a dead-end. To succeed, you must depart from the road that leads from great to grave, before it's too late.

Karaoke is Japanese for Empty (Kara) Orchestra (Oke). During the last few years we dealt with change by clearing out the orchestra, once called the strategic planning department, and replacing internal thinking with industry experts we share with our competitors. In effect, sameness rules. We believe that the time has come to re-unite the band – if the Police can do it, so can you. But, in business the repertoire requires radical revision. Planning won't work. Today, we face the challenge of creating an organization with leaders capable of re-energizing the future rather than managers clinging to re-iterating the truths of the past. We must lead with ideas and ideals.

# 8   The balancing act

## The pursuit of novelty

To enable positive surprise, corporations and leaders need a new point of departure. For starters, let's begin with what we actually know. Superstars are different. They know that, over time, all individuals, organizations and regions need to do exactly two things to survive and thrive. We must exploit our current competitive advantages while constantly innovating to come up with new ones – perform and transform. Exploitation ensures the effective utilization of existing resources and appropriation of value stemming from today's activities. Creation is aimed at seeking opportunities for the future.

We all need a combination of both. IBM moved from mainframes to PCs to consulting. Pablo Picasso went from blue to rose, from African-inspired painting to cubism over to neoclassicism and surrealism to reproductions of the other great masters of art.

Firms that fail to exploit newly created advantages will reap only the costs without gaining any of the returns. There's also a clear risk that such organizations will never attain critical mass in competences, markets or manufacturing. Corporations that have a too narrow focus on exploitation will, sooner or later, lose out to more innovative competitors. Today, we may as well erase later in the previous sentence.

Getting one out of these two basics right just doesn't do the trick. Think about Xerox. This firm is an amazing innovator, but historically it has also been an abysmal exploiter of all the technologies created at its PARC research lab. The same was largely true of Apple (which actually got off to a start after "borrowing" the GUI for its Macintosh from PARC) prior to the launch of its iMac, iPod and iMusic. In certain respects, the company still struggles because of its (Steve Jobs'?) obsession with controlling everything. Indeed, as sexy as it may be, Apple isn't on the list of the most profitable organizations in the world.

Most corporations, however, fail in innovation rather than exploitation. It's not only the history of pop-music which is littered with one hit wonders, like Rick Dee's *Disco Duck* from the 1970s or (for those a little younger) the absolutely unforgettable *Ice Ice Baby* by Vanilla Ice that topped the charts in 1990. The same is largely true for the business community. Far too many organizations die because they fail to come up with the sequel to their first blockbuster. From an overall economic perspective this may be OK. Some of the fastest growing regions actually have extreme levels of corporate mortality. If you're set to lead one of these organizations, however, the implications are quite different.

Exploitation and innovation compete for scarce resources. At a given point in time, in any corporation, there's only a fixed amount of time, a certain sum of money, limited cognitive capacity available, etc. – unless of course you can come up with innovative ways in which to provide a platform linked to a purpose that triggers the passion of people to participate on a volunteer basis like YouTube, Linux and OhMyNews. The repetition versus renewal battles of this corporate civil war rage on 24/7, 365 days a year. On top of that, there are many reasons why it's difficult to combine exploitation and innovation – to balance the needs for change and continuity. The first set of complications is related to the nature of man, whereas the second concern the organizational implications and requirements posed by the respective set of activities.

## On mice and men

There's a built-in resistance in most sane people to the unknown and uncertain. Few of us have that much in common with Bruce Willis' John McClane character in the *Die Hard* movies. When exposed to surprise we go "Yikes" instead of "Yippie-ka-yeah". We also know that the outcome of acts of creation or experimentation are less certain and obvious than those focused on exploitation and repetition. The consequences of such innovation-oriented activities are also more remote in time. So, since most people prefer to play it safe, we continue to exploit – day after day, year after year.

Research by Stanford's James March and Jonas' old mentor Gunnar Hedlund suggests that over time organizations learn how to allocate resources between the two types of activities. This balancing act has short-term as well as long-term effects. The feedback loops from activities where we focus on exploitation tend to be quicker and more precise. In effect, learning processes improve the productivity of exploitation oriented work more rapidly than is the case when we try to be disruptive and create something new. This, in turn, impacts on how we allocate our limited resources. The long-term effect is that exploitation crowds out and finally kills creation.

Just like the historical Greeks and Digital Equipment, most of today's organization will probably spend more and more of their resources exploiting the recipes of the past. If not re-energized, corporations and humans tend to become increasingly conservative and rigid in their behavior; more predictable and less likely to surprise the rest of us.

Now, take a break and fold your arms across your chest. Then, please unfold them. Next, fold them again across your chest, but force yourself to do it in a different way. It was a little bit more difficult, was it not? Yet, what we're asking you to do isn't exactly rocket science, is it? Think about when you put on your pants in the morning. You always start with the same leg. We all become captives of our past and held hostage by our historical routines.

This type of routinized behavior may not help you to thrive, but it does keep you alive. If you were to get an owner's manual to your body when you're born, the first chapter would be called survival. A bit like Arnold Schwarzenegger in the *Terminator* movies, we're all (biologically) programmed to stay alive rather than to enjoy the good life. You steer clear of death by avoiding risk and minimizing uncertainty. People and companies alike, therefore prefer to imitate rather than innovate. Copies abound while true originals are rare.

The challenge that we all face in a business world where increasingly the winners take all – like Microsoft and Google – is that those who are just too late or just too little seldom happen to be around for that long. The innovators get everything while the imitating losers are standing small. A leader taking on the task of making change happen by re-energizing the organization must therefore develop behaviors – their own and those of others – that often fly in the face of human nature. You must empower yourself and others to choose curiosity over absolute certainty, the potential for having a good life over just staying alive, and the odd chance of thriving over merely surviving. You must choose what's positive in the long run rather than just avoid the short-term negatives.

The challenge is further aggravated by the fact that the faster the world seems to be spinning, and the more novelty we're exposed to, the likelier we are to go for the safe bet. Surprise triggers instrumentality – predictable behavior in response to an unpredictable reality.

Think about how globalization increases uncertainty. Imagine that you're in New Delhi. You've just checked in at the *Le Meridien* hotel in the city center. Tomorrow morning, you're going to attend the most important business meeting of your career so far. Unfortunately, the food on the flight to India was terrible so you're really hungry. Since it's your first visit to Delhi you decide to leave your room and venture into the city for a culinary adventure. Walking down one of the streets you suddenly catch sight of them; to your left is Singh's Deli in Delhi and to your right you can see the familiar M of McDonald's. Where will you go? Remember that it's a really, really, really important business-meeting tomorrow.

Like the other 99.99967% of all non-Indians we've asked, we bet you would step right into the McDonald's restaurant. At McDonald's we know exactly what's on the menu; we know exactly what it's going to taste like; and we know exactly how disappointed we're going to be! But it's predictable.

Against this backdrop, we shouldn't be surprised that our past is awash with examples of companies that failed to surprise and delight us because they got trapped by their own success as exploiters of a particular competence combo. They stepped into a competency trap and found themselves stuck . . . in the past. Think Facit. Think of the British Empire. Think Ford, Chrysler and GM.

In 1990, IBM made $6 billion in profits. Three years later, the company posted an annual loss of $8 billion. Since then, IBM has made a great comeback – as have firms like Porsche and Puma during the same period. We love these examples. Boxers and business machines alike, it's never too late to change and surprise the rest of us. For those prepared to get on the change-train, there's still light at the end of the tunnel.

## Balancing your business

The second set of reasons for the permanence of the exploitation-innovation dilemma is related to the fact that the respective activities pose very different requirements on the overall architecture of the corporation. Neither organizationally nor strategically do change and continuity co-exist without causing considerable strain inside the company. Just think about the budgeting process. And then there are all the leadership challenges.

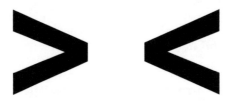

As we've noted, the ideal exploiter is set to perfect the known – repeating its magical formula over and over again. It operates under the assumption that its input, throughput and output is given and eternal. Therefore, this firm can adopt a hierarchical and bureaucratic organizational form to become a mean, money making efficiency machine churning out identical product after product. Think Henry Ford. Think Model T. Think any color so long it's black. Senior executives at headquarters act as resource-allocators and strategic decision makers. They plan, organize, command, coordinate and control. The rest of the organization, at home and abroad, implements what's handed over to them. Roles and responsibilities of people and units can be rigidly defined. This procedure also simplifies the friction-free exchange of workers at lower levels. You're dispensable.

Corporations focused on creating the unknown and unseen need to be organized in a radically different way. Innovation is usually the result of two different ideas from inside or outside the organization being brought together in an unexpected way. Creation of novelty will therefore require the kind of diversity of input that provides perspective as well as platforms and processes enabling combination of knowledge. These days, such processes often span individual, geographical, functional, or perhaps even institutional borders.

For decades, such processes have been commonplace in European companies like Philips and Electrolux. Now, this model for global innovation is spreading. Half of Microsoft's R&D labs are located outside the US and we find six of Toyota's seven R&D centers outside Japan. In Innovation Inc. exactly what competencies to pool will shift over time and depend on the circumstances. In effect, roles of individuals and units are more broadly defined. Temporary and boundary spanning project teams are the preferred modus operandi for the creating corporation – it's an adhocracy.

Since ideas can be born anywhere, the organizational and geographical location of leadership is also less permanent. At Creation Corp., it's based on your capacity for idea generation and consequent resource-attraction rather than the formal right to take decisions about the allocation of resources. Executives are reborn as catalysts and coaches for X-men and X-women working across boundaries and borders. HQ becomes a servant to the rest of the organization. At the highly successful South African fast food restaurant chain Nando's, headquarters is even labeled *central support*.

## Manuscript or improvizational theater?

The predictable nature of the sources underlying competitiveness in the exploiting organization also implies that it can rely on standardization and planning to coordinate activities. Efficiency and consistency is ensured by the use of formalized procedures and adherence to the chain-of-command. Historically, US and Japanese multinationals were often run like this. Think recipe. Think Coke and McDonald's.

Organizations set to produce surprise need a more informal approach based on mutual adjustment. The preferred future outcome of its processes is just too uncertain for a manual to provide all the answers. Since ideas and needs could very well be separated across geography and the organization, communication-flows must be horizontal as much as vertical. Socialization in terms of having people spend a lot of time together with different colleagues becomes critical. "Innovation through combination" makes "know-who" just as important as, or perhaps even more critical than individual "know-how". Also remember that tacit knowledge – the kind of knowledge that exists between people who have been together for years and years, like Bono and the Edge of U2 or Bill and Steve of Microsoft – enables us to communicate without using words and is much more difficult for the competition to imitate. Shared beliefs, norms and values keep the organization from complete chaos and utter anarchy. These fundamentals, in turn, are sometimes reinforced by international rotation and (temporary) co-location of people.

## Competence complexity

The productivity-disruptivity paradox faces all organizations but, as argued by Gunnar Hedlund, the challenges become more pronounced the more the network of competencies that the corporation needs to utilize in the pursuit of new competitive advantages is characterized by high levels of knowledge intensity and extensity. The patterns left by historical strategic actions provide all organizations with a position along these two dimensions. Here, it's impossible not to have a position.

|  | **Extensity** | |
|---|---|---|
|  | Low | High |
| **High** | "Silicon Valley" | "Transnational Professional" |
| **Low** | "Business as Usual" | "Global Recipe" |

Knowledge intensity is a term used by most people in a familiar and loose way. We all seem to sort of know what it means. In our opinion, networks of corporate competences can be intense in two very different ways. Intensity potentially relates to both the *depth* and the *durability* of competencies. Competition forces fashion companies like H&M or Zara to come up with new collections at least twice per year and new products just about every day. These organizations are tremendously successful but don't employ huge numbers of university professors. Compare that to the situation in the pharmaceutical industry. Patents still provide a decent form of protection, but in order to ensure long-term success, firms need to come up with a new block-buster drug every five years or so. While the economic durability of products is longer, high-intensity firms in industries with increased calls for knowledge depth are heavily reliant on a gang of nerds, geeks, weirdos, whacky whizz-kids, nutty professors and other oddballs. IBM Labs, for instance, employs more than 2000 PhDs and has six Nobel Laureates on its pay roll. How many universities can match that?

Companies that rely heavily on well-educated employees, not only at the top, and those active in industries with short product life-cycles more or less by definition need to move beyond solutions relying on rigid hierarchical control. Name one successful player in the biotech or IT-telecom industries that gets away with bureaucratic structures and a corporate rule-book inspired by Joe Stalin.

Knowledge extensity also complicates things. Companies relying on more than one home-base in developing their competitive edge face the extensity challenge from a *dispersion* point of view. So do those that have to combine many different technologies or skills, but from a *diversity* perspective. No matter what, these corporations will experience nervous breakdowns if they try to squeeze all this complexity into an organizational architecture equivalent to the pyramid of Cheops.

Think about Sony. It's headquartered in Japan and the US, and also has strategically important units in Europe. The firm relies heavily on a global network of suppliers. For instance, all of its LCD flat-screen panels are supplied by a 50/50 joint-venture with its sworn enemy, Samsung. This is akin to the political developments in Northern Ireland. In its mobile phone joint-venture with Ericsson, Sony faces the challenge of merging technologies resulting in products that are phones + PDAs + cameras + movie players + game consoles + Walkmans + etc. with Internet access. In doing so, the firm also directly competes with many of its own traditional products. Imagination is the only limit.

Technologies converge. Fact. As knowledge spreads, the earth gets flatter. Often, dispersion and diversity go hand in hand. What do you think are the odds that one of the world's recent university graduates is a white male? Answer: 1 in 5. In the future, an increasing number of firms will have to deal with the extensity challenge. For many, the consequences of internationalization and increased calls for hyphenation are already business as usual.

Calculate your own corporate competence profile in the figure below by marking your position compared to your two toughest competitors with x, y and z on the dotted line. Then think about the following questions:

- How do you match up – are you more or less sophisticated than the rest?
- What does your relative position imply from a strategy point of view – strengths and weakness?
- What type of threats and opportunities do you face?
- Which position would make you absolutely unique from a corporate competence perspective?
- Why is no one already there?

Next, use a circle to denote where you need to be five years from now. Here are another couple of questions:

- Why will you have to get there?
- How will you get there?

- How will you get people on board?
- Who will be responsible for making it happen?
- What are the consequences from an organizational, managerial and leadership point of view?
- In what ways will these strategic moves add value to stakeholders inside and outside the firm?
- What are you competitors likely to do?

Even if your organization's current network of competences is neither that intensive nor overtly extensive, remember that those that revolutionize industries typically do so by initiating activities that change the rules of the game by boosting either the intensity or the extensity (or both) of their position vis-à-vis competition. Vodaphone did it in the telecommunications sector. IKEA changed the furniture business. Starbucks re-invented its industry. You can re-energize yours. "Never doubt that a small group of thoughtful, committed citizens can change the world. Indeed, it is the only thing that ever has," observes the author, Margaret Mead.

## Knowledge Intensity

Low                                  Medium                                  High

share of employees with Ph.D. degree

. . . . . . . . . . . . . . . . . . . . . . . . . . . . . . . . . . . . . . . . . . . . . . . . . . . . . .

share of sales spent on training and education

. . . . . . . . . . . . . . . . . . . . . . . . . . . . . . . . . . . . . . . . . . . . . . . . . . . . . .

share of sales spent on research and development

. . . . . . . . . . . . . . . . . . . . . . . . . . . . . . . . . . . . . . . . . . . . . . . . . . . . . .

share of employees receiving yearly training and education

. . . . . . . . . . . . . . . . . . . . . . . . . . . . . . . . . . . . . . . . . . . . . . . . . . . . . .

share of employees who need to upgrade their skills every year to stay competitive

. . . . . . . . . . . . . . . . . . . . . . . . . . . . . . . . . . . . . . . . . . . . . . . . . . . . . .

share of administrative systems and procedures introduced in the last two years

. . . . . . . . . . . . . . . . . . . . . . . . . . . . . . . . . . . . . . . . . . . . . . . . . . . . . .

share of administrative systems and procedures introduced in the last five years

. . . . . . . . . . . . . . . . . . . . . . . . . . . . . . . . . . . . . . . . . . . . . . . . . . . . . .

share of sales from customer offerings introduced in the last two years

. . . . . . . . . . . . . . . . . . . . . . . . . . . . . . . . . . . . . . . . . . . . . . . . . . . . . .

share of sales from customer offerings introduced in the last five years

. . . . . . . . . . . . . . . . . . . . . . . . . . . . . . . . . . . . . . . . . . . . . . . . . . . . . .

## Knowledge Extensity

Low                                        Medium                                        High

share of employees outside the home country

. . . . . . . . . . . . . . . . . . . . . . . . . . . . . . . . . . . . . . . . . . . . . . . . . . . . . . . .

share of research and development outside the home country

. . . . . . . . . . . . . . . . . . . . . . . . . . . . . . . . . . . . . . . . . . . . . . . . . . . . . . . .

share of production outside the home country

. . . . . . . . . . . . . . . . . . . . . . . . . . . . . . . . . . . . . . . . . . . . . . . . . . . . . . . .

share of suppliers outside the home country

. . . . . . . . . . . . . . . . . . . . . . . . . . . . . . . . . . . . . . . . . . . . . . . . . . . . . . . .

share of sales outside the home country

. . . . . . . . . . . . . . . . . . . . . . . . . . . . . . . . . . . . . . . . . . . . . . . . . . . . . . . .

share of innovation projects involving collaboration across functions

. . . . . . . . . . . . . . . . . . . . . . . . . . . . . . . . . . . . . . . . . . . . . . . . . . . . . . . .

share of innovation projects involving collaboration across business
areas

. . . . . . . . . . . . . . . . . . . . . . . . . . . . . . . . . . . . . . . . . . . . . . . . . . . . . . . .

share of innovation projects involving collaboration across nations

. . . . . . . . . . . . . . . . . . . . . . . . . . . . . . . . . . . . . . . . . . . . . . . . . . . . . . . .

share of innovation projects involving collaboration with external
partners

. . . . . . . . . . . . . . . . . . . . . . . . . . . . . . . . . . . . . . . . . . . . . . . . . . . . . . . .

# 9 Split decision

## Seasons in the sun

Since exploitation and innovation don't exactly go together like a horse and carriage, there seems to be good reasons for keeping them apart. Potentially, companies could decide to separate these activities over both time and space. Let's begin by taking a closer look at the pros and cons of the former.

By sequencing creation and exploitation over time some of the difficulties that we've discussed could be avoided. The organization would focus its strategic attention on creating new advantages under one period and then gradually move on to exploit these and subsequently enter a new phase of innovation, etc. The corporation would essentially have two different seasons that come and go.

This cyclical approach posits an industry with routinized and almost institutionalized "big leap" type of innovations, where considerable time passes between the introductions of new major product generations. We've seen many examples of the procedure being used by companies, particularly in business to business cases where there appears to be a tacit agreement – a shared industry-wide business recipe – between all major competitors that new products are supposed to be introduced every five or ten years. In some of these cases, the main reason for shifting focus from exploitation to innovation was determined by the pay-back time of the old investments rather than new technological opportunities or shifting customer demand. In some industries, cost, rather than the customer, is king.

The key risk associated with this separation over time model for managing the paradox is that someone, and often an outsider, enters the business with a completely new logic, cutting development and lead time. Nokia did it the telecommunications industry by flooding the market with new mobiles at a rate that no other company could keep up with. The Japanese did very much the same thing in the automotive industry. Another dilemma is having more or less all activities centered on exploitation during an extended period which limits the scope for continuous process improvements.

Practical problems with sequencing also apply to the people aspect of the equation. How many of your colleagues are capable of performing both types of activities? And even if they have the skills, can they shift mindset from one time to another? Will those in charge of the more temporary innovation process have the necessary organizational clout and legitimacy or will not loyalty rest with executives from the operating organization of "yesterday and tomorrow"? It's our experience that most people pledge allegiance to those who set their salaries and have the final say on promotions. Featherweight project managers are usually no match for Sumo execs.

## Give me space

Separation across space is the second strategy for dealing with the innovation-exploitation dilemma. As illustrated in the table below, corporations can implement this arrangement on the institutional, geographical, organizational and individual level. In Jonas' earlier work with Gunnar Hedlund, they made the argument that these choices have clear implications for what overall strategy the organization can pursue and what type of innovations we should expect. In general, the lower the level of internal separation of exploitation and creation the more incremental and evolutionary stuff will be the result. Higher levels of separation generally imply more revolutionary and radical innovations, except in those industries where big leaps require (re-)combination of knowledge.

| Separation – Level / Degree | Low | High |
|---|---|---|
| **Institutional space** | Generalists | Specialists |
| **Geographical space** | Polycentric | Ethnocentric |
| **Organizational space** | Rugby | Relay |
| **Individual space** | McGyver | Homes & Watson |

# Hollower than thou?

Organizations may decide to go for a high-separation strategy across institutional space by focusing on only one type of activity and leaving the rest to partners – suppliers, customers or at times even competitors – in the environment. Today, arrangements for outsourcing exploitation to low-cost producers are commonplace, but an increasing number of firms also farm out creation. Cisco Systems, for instance, has in many respects outsourced innovation to smaller and more entrepreneurial companies. From the acquisition of Crescendo Communications in 1993 to Web Ex in 2007, the company has been able to exploit ideas developed somewhere else by someone else by using its own well-oiled distribution system. Other corporations, like Dell, Motorola and Philips simply buy complete designs of certain digital devices from Asian developers. Many Western titans of business now orchestrate external innovation networks with global reach.

For those that off-shore innovation, there are risks associated with the brand losing some of its flair once people figure this out. The procedure also adds little or no uniqueness if your competitors shop at the same store. For firms using the acquisition oriented approach, potential scale economies in R&D are lost. The biggest challenge, however, has to do with the fact that it's difficult to dissociate competence from its use. Research suggests that technological development is a process that's mostly cumulative, tacit and firm-specific. Without that knowledge, how would you be able to spot potentially successful innovations? Where would you look and what would you look for?

# Ethoncentric or polycentric?

The second level at which separation can take place refers to geographical space. Work by Harvard's Chris Bartlett and the late Sumantra Ghoshal from London Business School shows that historically two archetypal models were dominant. European multinationals, and particularly those from small countries like Holland and Sweden, such as Unilever and Electrolux, adopted a polycentric model with limited separation. Here, many units had the capabilities to both exploit and create. Most US and Japanese firms, on the other hand, preferred a more ethnocentric solution, with clear separation between what happens at headquarters and foreign subsidiaries, respectively. Firms like Matsushita and GE used to innovate at home and exploit abroad.

Both solutions come with advantages and disadvantages. Low separation across geographical space typically worked better in industries with great requirements for local responsiveness, whereas organizations applying a high separation approach generally did better in industries with an emphasis on global efficiency. Polycentric firms may risk reinventing the wheel, again losing out on scale economies in R&D. Ethnocentric ones often suffer from not being able to take advantage of the fact that the source of particularly process innovation is often to be found in exploitation, which here is located elsewhere. Then there are of course also the motivational consequences of being assigned the role of merely being an implementer, rather than a leader, to consider. The lack of local entrepreneurship or rebellious Not-Invented-Here reactions are common symptoms of the drawbacks related to centralizing innovation by concentrating it to only one location.

Yet, the biggest challenge, regardless of what extreme solution you apply, rests with the fact that in most modern industries success requires that you're both locally responsive *and* globally efficient. Merely getting one of the two requirements right is no longer enough.

## All for one or one for all?

The next level of separation concerns organizational space. High separation would typically mean giving one function – and in 99.9% of the cases this would be R&D – prime responsibility for creation. This procedure means that innovation equals technology push, with clearly defined responsibilities for "star and dog" departments. The sequential relay-approach that follows from this way of operating implies that R&D creates and then hands over the baton to manufacturing that finally passes it on to marketing and sales for exploitation. This approach was – and is – still popular in most Western corporations. A more concurrent engineering-oriented and rugby-like approach is based on less separation of exploitation and creation across functions. Innovation occurs in cross-functional teams that are manned by people not only from R&D. Many Japanese firms, like Toyota and Canon, are pioneers in using such arrangements.

The first approach can result in big break-throughs but often runs the risk of triggering the Not-Invented-Here syndrome, especially in the marketing and sales organization. Technology push can and has also, on more than one occasion, resulted in fantastic sci-fi products without any real demand. Many a company has been forced to file for bankruptcy after having spent years and years building a better mouse-trap.

Similarly, the rugby approach isn't without drawbacks. The administrative costs of this solution can be enormous, particularly in a company not used to collaboration across functions. Moreover, the result of such (negotiation) processes is rarely big-leap innovations that wow the world.

In multinationals, the challenges are also aggravated by variations in the location patterns of the principal departments in question. R&D, which is still in most corporations concentrated to one or just a few locations, will push for global standardization. Marketing which is usually spread all over the space, will argue for local adaptation. Manufacturing is generally (caught) somewhere in between. The end-result is always spelt conflict.

## Is there an I in your team?

Finally, there are issues relating to separation over individual space. Low levels of separation means relying on corporate renaissance men (and women) with a capability to both exploit and create – envision and execute. Think American adventurer *MacGyver*, played by Richard Dean Anderson in the 1980s television series. According to Wikipedia, Angus MacGyver's key asset "is his practical application of scientific knowledge and inventive use of common items – along with his ever-present Swiss Army knife and duct tape and the usual coincidence of being locked up in a room full of useful materials. The clever solutions MacGyver implemented to seemingly intractable problems – often in life-or-death situations requiring him to improvise complex devices in a matter of minutes – were a major attraction of the show, which was praised for generating interest in engineering as well as providing entertaining storylines." To produce corporate men and women of that caliber careers would have to be generalist where people move horizontally as well as vertically.

Higher levels of separation more resemble a "Holmes and Watson" model with specialist careers and deep rather than broad knowledge. Again, according to Wikipedia, Sherlock Holmes is "a brilliant London-based detective . . . famous for his intellectual prowess, and is renowned for his skillful use of deductive reasoning (somewhat mistakenly) and astute observation to solve difficult cases . . . Dr. John H. Watson isn't a stupid man (he is, after all, a medical doctor, and one whose talents Holmes holds in the highest esteem), but he doesn't have Holmes' insight. He serves as a foil to Holmes: the ordinary man against the brilliant, emotionally-detached analytical machine that Holmes can sometimes be." When we separate exploitation and creation on the individual level, some will focus on thinking and others will have to settle for doing.

The first approach may be accused of being slightly utopist – McGyver was after all a fictional character (OK, so were Holmes and Watson). Even in our times of talent, the supply of renaissance people is kind of scarce. But also the solution with a more strict division of labor is problematic. Worker dissatisfaction could very well countervail any gains in efficiency and learning from increased specialization. Who knows, after the "You-volution", Watson may actually tell Holmes to go . . . himself and simply walk away.

## The choice is yours

Handling the dual demands for exploitation and creation isn't an impossible dream. There are things that we can do. Yet, we promise that any search for a final structural solution which ensures that you're the surprise of your industry will be in vain. Division rarely produces an output greater than the input. Multiplication mostly does. To get there, however, your corporation needs an organizational architecture supportive of re-energizing.

Before we move on to show how re-energizing leadership can make a difference in dealing with the innovation-exploitation dilemma, go back to the table covering the effects of separating or not separating the two basic types of activities that are necessary for ensuring organizational survival. Most organizations will of course have less straight profiles, but still take some time and think about the following:

- What's the relative position of your organization in these dimensions?
- Were the choices behind your separation profile actively made or did they just happen organically?
- How well aligned are the positions on the different levels of your profile?
- How does it differ from those of your competitors?
- Which type of innovation should you expect from these corporations?
- What does the future hold for you?

## 10 The people power plant

### Albert the Barbarian

Sad but true, too many companies are managed by people in whom the traits of Albert Einstein and Conan the Barbarian come together. We're not the first to arrive at this conclusion. More than 20 years ago, Harvard's leadership guru John Kotter noted that most unsuccessful companies (and as you know by now, sorry to say, these are a dime a dozen) suffer from the unfortunate combination of simultaneously being over-managed and under-led. From a corporate survival and success point of view, this combo is kind of akin to being led by someone having Albert's body and Conan's brain. John Kotter's statement still holds true. By now it should be evident that we're convinced that more traditional 20th century management will not get you anywhere closer to being the positive surprise that your corporation wants and has to be in a world of change and competition.

The appropriate response to the 21st century corporate challenge isn't more management, but a new approach to leadership – not excluding all traditional managerial responsibilities because some of these are indeed important aspects of a re-energizing leadership style. To succeed, we need both an overall organizational architecture enabling and supporting leaders in re-energizing the corporation and practical tools for selecting, screening, evaluating and developing leaders in the three core processes of envisioning, engaging and executing. In the remainder of this part, we'll focus of the former task.

### The architecture of change

The organizational architecture of a corporation is important in conditioning the success and failure of projects and individual efforts aimed at creating opportunities for the future. In our research and consulting work we've met many leaders who have turned to us after bombing not because they were terrible at leading specific re-energizing processes, but since they had failed to realize that all change efforts, processes and projects take place in a context – cultural, structural and historical. Companies carry around the baggage of an administrative heritage. There just is no escape. And without a fertile ground, most seeds of surprise and initiatives to energize will wither and die.

In the following chapters, we'll outline three pillars of an organizational architecture for renewal – a people power-plant. All arrangements are aimed at maximizing the value of your organization's intellectual, psychological and social capital. Anyone claiming to provide you with a blueprint for how to build such a firm is taking on a Herculean task. We can only but give you a rough sketch of such an architecture. Don't worry. If, in this book, we could give you a detailed drawing, your competitors would also have access to it and it would, as a result, be commercially worthless.

## Expanding the energy force-field

In our work with organization we generally distinguish between four basic energy conversion modes;

- Physical: working harder
- Professional: working smarter
- Psychological: working heartier
- Processual: working together (in ways enabling the whole to be greater than the sum of the parts)

Our primary interest is focused on the three latter aspects. By now, in all probability, in your industry the physical part of the conversion process is increasingly up to the Chinese, Indians or East Europeans. We also think it's crucial that the overall framework for re-energizing the firm enables a greater: *focus* – people should do what they are good at and passionate about, more *fusion* – processes that make the most out of intellectual diversity, *fission* – creation-oriented innovation projects that are separated and protected from the exploitation-focused core of the firm, and reduce *friction* – barriers to communication, creativity and the ability to produce change.

This is the challenge. Corporations need to introduce methods that enable people everywhere in the organization to utilize their individual creative and emotional potential to the fullest. Yet, at the same time, organizations must also take measures ensuring that individual freedom is combined with an ability to take collective action – me and we need to co-exist.

The objective of the following chapters is therefore to aid you in building an organization based on fantasy, feelings and faith – a place where it's OK to imagine, sense and behave as a positive deviant. To succeed in taking people on this journey, you'll need to develop protean capabilities and act as part professor, part psychologist and part priest. Re-energizing concerns the cognition and emotion as well as locomotion of people and organizations. Your challenge as a leader set to re-energize is therefore to guide your team on the road from the competence campus to the confidence clinic and into the courage cathedral, thereby making change happen. Think – feel – do – then, rinse, repeat.

## The million dollar questions

Our future, collectively and individually, is a little bit like death. No one has ever come back with a completely reliable report about what it's like there on the other side – not even (certainly not?) American TV-evangelists like the late Jerry Falwell. What we do know, however, after years and years spent working with leaders and companies on these issues, is that the future is fundamentally driven by questions, much more so than by the answers we already hold. Answers produce predictability. Questions give rise to surprise. In the following, we'll therefore focus on the three basic questions that all leaders who want to re-energize their business must figure out the answer to:

- Why do we/I need to change?
- Why should we/I care?
- Why should we/I contribute?

To further complicate things, already at this point, let's point out that the hypothesis that you and your confidants arrive at have to make sense not only to you, but also to folks around you. Annoying as they may be from time to time, these persons happen to be exactly the people who will keep on asking you questions – over and over again.

# 11 Constructing the competence campus

## Back to the future

To flourish in a world of change – to be the surprise – you must first begin to understand what drives this transformation. What are the main reasons behind the seismic shift toward a society in which stability has been replaced by surprise? Again, don't worry. In one sense, there isn't anything mysterious or strange about the forces that are currently re-shaping the business landscape. Three eternal forces have always influenced and will continue to affect the basic conditions for success in life in general and business life in particular. When we – mankind – develop new technologies, launch innovative institutional arrangements and when fresh values evolve our world changes.

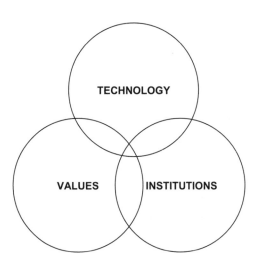

In our experience, far too few companies and executives spend a sufficient amount of time and energy thinking about how these fundamental forces and changes might affect their businesses right now and even more so five or ten years down the road. They take the overall socio-economic context for given, or just put on blinders preventing them from seeing what's really going on. Do you? Just think about some of the critical dimensions. In 2013:

- **Portfolio:** What products and services will you live on?
- **Pipeline:** How and when will these be developed?
- **Positioning:** You'll sell them to the following customers?
- **Place:** They will be delivered through the following channel(s)?
- **Passion:** For the following reasons, you'll give people goosebumps?
- **Priorities:** To be distinct you'll say yes and no, respectively, to the following things at these points in time?

As we've emphasized, time and time again, unless you do something about it, exploitation crowds out creation and eventually kills it. Keep in mind that an opportunity not acted upon has a nasty habit of eventually becoming a threat. And problems don't age that well. Also note that when referring to envisioning, we're not talking about stargazing or urging you to look into a veritable crystal-ball. Re-energizing your leadership isn't about becoming the Oracle of Delphi or Merlin the magician of your firm. Our experience is that, quite often, just stating some basic facts about simple things that we already know a lot about, such as changing demographics outside and inside the firm, is enough to fuel an interesting and heated debate.

## The entrepreneurial sociologist

Why, in an unpredictable world, is all this talk about preparing for tomorrow important then? Well, great entrepreneurs – from Leonardo Da Vinci to Thomas Alva Edison and the coffee-evangelist Howard Schultz – have always been not only great artists, inventors and business-minds. Above all, they have proved to be some pretty awesome sociologists. "Paying attention to simple little things that most men neglect makes a few men rich," said Henry Ford. These people simply possess and are obsessed with what Josef Schumpeter once labeled "combinative capabilities." They excel at integrating knowledge from one field with ideas from another. We call this socio-economic arbitrage – foresight by insight.

Such arbitrage opportunities exist across *levels, functions and space/ time*. Transfer recipes from the organizational world to the individual level – get a second job and out-source your work to India. Bring in a conductor to teach business leaders about performance management. Have some Silicon Valley entrepreneurs energize a region in Croatia by exposing people to the future. By using your intellect to connect the dots already present on the firmament of human development, progress and evolution, you can anticipate tomorrow's opportunities.

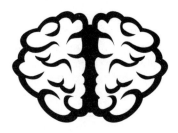

In the following, we'll focus on how the current changes impact on how you'll have to deal with people both inside and outside your organization. Why? It's deceptively simple. Leaders, as we see them, are mediators between the talent of the company's employees and the desires that the customers of the corporation have. To be a value-adding link in this relationship, leaders need to maximize the utilization of their IC.

Succeeding in this first phase of re-energizing requires that you keep on asking the questions of why and in what respects the world and its people – customers, competents and capitalists – are changing. You have to do this in order to figure out what will become scarce and in demand. WHY = WHAT'S NEXT. Then, think why not. Starting next Monday, set aside more time to think creatively about the future. Surprise is dependent on many things but it's always contingent on slack. There are reasons for why a company such as Google requires all its engineers to spend 20% of their time working on their own projects. The first step in developing into a re-energizing leader of change therefore requires that you become more of a slacker! Here, we can only give you a few hints about what you and your team may want to think and talk about tomorrow morning.

## Join the freedom-fighters

Historically, technology was used to manipulate and control people into mindless submission and consumption. Now, it sets us free. These days, technology works for the people. With new phenomena such as the Internet and mobile phones, the business world has never been neither bigger nor smaller. Today, total global competition goes on everywhere, non-stop and at the same time your worst competitor is never more than a couple of clicks away. Think about the millions of YouTubers and MySpacers. Think about the tens of thousands of Indian IT-engineers who do work for companies located in the West. These people are virtual immigrants. Also think about Lorna who used to be called Steve before her (his?) sex-change operation. How can you make these forces work for rather than against you?

At the same time, traditional institutions are crumbling. With the high divorce rates that we see in many parts of the world, should we really expect that anyone is willing to pledge allegiance to one company and one boss for the rest of their lives? What happens to the employer-employee deal when most people should expect to out-live the company that they are currently working for? What are the economic and social implications of the fact that many high-growth regions like Silicon Valley also score extremely high on corporate mortality? What does it mean when more people vote before the final episode of Big Brother and American Idol than in the elections to Parliament? We're not making this up. Facts are at times stranger than fiction. But facts never lie. What's in this for you?

Similarly, in terms of values, the meaning of life has been joined by the meaning of "lite". How do you deal with the fact that fewer and fewer people work out of moral obligations, like our parents did? Try to find anyone who believes that poorly paid, dangerous and mind-numbing work is worth doing simply because it cleanses the soul. Our world is becoming increasingly *Paris Hiltonificated*. Fame is no longer necessarily based on what you've done, as it used to be. Now, you can be famous also for just being famous. Welcome to the age of appearance. We style ourselves, our bodies and our homes.

More and more people do just about anything to get their 15 minutes of fame. Have sex with a celebrity, like Divine Brown joining English actor Hugh Grant – become famous for being with the famous. (No, we're not going to bring up Ms. Lewinsky again.) Or boost your celebrity, like Pam Anderson and Tommy Lee or Paris Hilton in *One Night in Paris* – by filming yourself having sex and become even more famous for being famous.

Also consider the fact that now for many people, tribal belonging is more related to purpose than place. Religions, culture and national origins mix. Today, think of your potential customers as members of the People's Republic of Justin Timberlake rather than French or Chinese. Biography is beginning to rival geography. So, what's the purpose of the tribe that you're targeting? Do you achieve and appear on a level high enough to get through?

## The real reality

Love them or hate them. Depeche Mode was right; people are people! But get this. Like it or not. These are your new customers. These are your new shareholders. These are your new colleagues. These are the people who you must re-energize. And believe it or not, in many respects, you're probably quite similar to them. Otherwise, we suspect that you wouldn't have gotten this far into the book. Like Neo in the *Matrix* movie, we all face a choice – deny reality or embrace it. You've already decided, aware of it or not, to take the red pill.

---

### The Matrix by Andy & Larry Wachowski

**Morpheus:** Let me tell you why you're here. You're here because you know something. What you know, you can't explain. But you feel it. You felt it your entire life. That there's something wrong with the world. You don't know what it is, but it's there. Like a splinter in your mind – driving you mad. It is this feeling that has brought you to me. Do you know what I'm talking about?

**Neo:** The Matrix?

**Morpheus:** Do you want to know what it is? (Neo nods)

**Morpheus:** The Matrix is everywhere, it is all around us. Even now, in this very room. You can see it when you look out your window, or when you turn on your television. You can feel it when you go to work, or when go to church or when you pay your taxes. It is the world that has been pulled over your eyes to blind you from the truth.

**Neo:** What truth?

**Morpheus:** That you are a slave, Neo. Like everyone else, you were born into bondage, born inside a prison that you can't smell, taste, or touch. A prison for your mind. Unfortunately, no one can be told what the Matrix is. You have to see it for yourself. This is your last chance. After this, there is no turning back. (Morpheus shows a blue pill.)

**Morpheus:** You take the blue pill and the story ends. You wake in your bed and believe whatever you want to believe.

---

> (Morpheus shows a red pill in his other hand) You take the red
> pill and you stay in Wonderland and I show you how deep the
> rabbit-hole goes. (Neo reaches for the red pill) Remember – all
> I am offering is the truth, nothing more.
>
> (Neo takes the red pill and swallows it down with a glass of
> water)

The current changes in technology, institutions and values have opened
up for the greatest freedom movement ever to hit planet Earth. We may
not be seeing huge hoards of people taking to the streets in protest or
going on mass-strike as we did during the 1960s, but instead people
travel the world as never before, blog to reach persons they don't really
know, practice serial monogamy or just simply believe in both God and
Gucci at the same time. These basic forces of change now interact in a
way that has given rise to two deregulation processes that are altering
the very nature of both the inner and the outer context in which we've
to lead our organizations. We're deregulating life as well as business
life. And, more freedom equals more . . . SURPRISE!

## And the winners are . . .

Consider the last 60 years of human history. Clearly, the post WWII period
has been marked by enormous efforts to give both people and corporations new rights of utterly unprecedented historical proportions. This
movement started out small and local in the Western world. Since then it
has spread around the globe like an almost unstoppable virus. Every once
in a while the immune system of conservatism and narrow-mindedness
kicks in. Think Tiananmen Square, Saddam, Pyong-Yang, Rush Limbaugh
and Jurg Haider. But once you've opened up the floodgates for existential
and economic freedom, there really is no going back.

After the collapse of communism, the rise and fall and then great
come-back of dot-communism, individualism and capitalism are if not
the only isms left on our planet, at least pretty high up on the top-ten
list of the early 21st century (unfortunately, so are fundamentalism and
extremism). The implications that follow from this revolution are crystal
clear – for Coldplay, the Pope in Rome, Angela Merkel and for you –
albeit, apparently not for Al-Qaida. In a world with new or perhaps even
no rules, those who thrive on freedom – personal and mercantile – will
rule the world. The new business reality is one dominated by man and
markets.

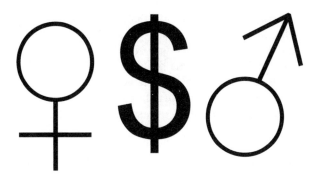

Freedom is a nice little word. Again, this is another term which is used in a loose and non-consequential kind of way by most of us. Unless regularly hanging out with the likes of Osama and Kim-Jung-Il, you rarely meet people who are 100%, totally, completely, and absolutely against the general concept. Personal freedom rocks! But, and it's a major *but*, when we urge executives to think about the freedom that their gold-collar employees currently have to quit and set up their own shop, for their most profitable customers to spend their money elsewhere, or for investors to shift their holdings by just pressing a button on their PC, most of them get a somewhat more worried look on their face.

Axiom: the more freedom people around you enjoy, the greater your responsibilities as a leader will become. In our topsy-turvy times, the triumph of this ferocious freedom movement creates a number of mega-challenges for the modern leader. Find comfort then in the fact that freedom of choice, which can be good and bad, is always better than no freedom of choice, which can only be bad.

## Existential freedom

American futurist and thinker Watts Wacker writes about the four basic rights that an increasing number of people now enjoy; the freedom to **know**, **go**, **do** and **be** whoever they want to be. Do you want to know some more? Google it. Ten years ago, you could not do that. Do you want to go somewhere? Jump on a flight with EasyJet, Ryan Air, or German Wings. Travel with South West Airlines or Air Asia. All over the world, these low-cost airlines will take you to most places for almost nothing. We're on the move. Right now, there are some 178 million migrants on our planet.

When we hand over power to the people, leaders will have to have a point of view about how to deal with a number of issues that they did not have to face 20–25 years ago. NO POV = NO WOW! And if we have indeed deregulated life, don't be surprised that we experience more surprise. People are now free to behave differently. So we do! The winners will therefore be those that facilitate this process by enabling people to conquer freedom and express their individuality.

## Will you democratize, meritocratize or mediocratize?

The climate has changed. You can't open a newspaper without reading at least one article about global warming. We've manipulated the environment to an extent that it now is beginning to strike back. The same phenomenon is noticeable also in our business environment. In nature, we measure temperature in either Fahrenheit or Celsius, and the temperature is rising. The equivalent measure from an economic point of view is the amount of information that we pump out to the citizens of this world. And that amount has been on a steady rise during the last 50 years. So, don't be astonished by the fact that people now are beginning to strike back. Star Wars may have brought the Soviet Union to its knees, but the final blow that eventually put a stop to this evil empire was the tsunami of information that was flooding the entire Eastern Bloc.

We issue a global warning to all those who believe that leadership power can be based on an information access monopoly. This simply won't work when people are free to know, go, do and be. With 40 000 new blogs added to the Internet every day, after the launch and growth of YouTube, with 24/7 CNN and Bloomberg, the 21st century business world is just too transparent for that old method to be effective. The answer is never more than a click away.

From this development follows a number of implications. Number 1. There's nowhere to run and nowhere to hide. Have you ever tried to find shelter after an unethical adventure? Ask anyone from Richard Milhaus Nixon to William Jefferson Clinton how easy it is. The harder they come the harder they fall. Have you insured your company against reputational risk? How would you go about doing it? Damage control is best done before the damage is done. Think Enron. Behave.

Number 2. Hanging on to the belief that you can bully yourself into success, pretending to have all the answers, is even more stupid. Dictators of the world – good bye! From an information point of view, our world is finally becoming democratized. So, as a leader you're facing a vital choice; deal with the new reality by meritocratizing your firm or watch it mediocratize. This also means admitting that you're not always right. Here's a little exercise for all our male readers. Try to say the following four words; I DO NOT KNOW.

Don't, however, fall into the trap of resignation, believing that more information in the hands of others necessarily implies less power for you. On the contrary, the more info spreads the more important knowledge and wisdom become. Right now, inside and outside your corporation, there are plenty of people who potentially can access all the information in the world. But since many of them lack the intellectual map and compass enabling them to make sense of it, things just don't make sense. This is a great opportunity for true leaders to leave their mark. How much of a sense-maker are you and the rest of your executive team? You're not planning to control people by keeping them in a "state of nonsense," are you?

In reality, what would meritocratization mean? Internally, the logical consequence means handing over more power from those with titles to those with talent. Mind you, in our experience most people are talented, but at different times and in various situations. Yesterday, corporations were inhabited by bosses and subordinates. Today, we're all "bossubordinates." From time to time this procedure probably means that in order to get going you'll have to let go. To surprise and survive, you'll depend on new voices. Intellectual diversity is a prerequisite for innovative combinations of knowledge to come about. Democratization of information forces you to lead with ideas rather than formal authority – your own ideas and those of others. But to ensure that your organization takes the lead you must still lead.

Intellectual leadership is all about initiating and facilitating a discussion that enables the organization to formulate and form around new challenges. Talent is accountable not to the strategist but to realizing the strategy – your shared purpose rather than a specific person. Dictators are therefore replaced by those who can dictate the rules of the debate that drives the dream forward – Osama has to surrender to Oprah.

Big Q: How Oprah are you?

Here are some other big Qs:

- In your company, do you have a sufficient number of marketplaces – real and virtual – for ideas?
- How many voices are heard and really listened to during your average management meeting?
- Do you regularly invite dissidents to get some fresh input?
- How often do suppliers and customers attend your get-togethers?
- Are ideas from the periphery given the same treatment as those from the center or does the corporate immune system at headquarters automatically reject them?

- Do you have enough corporate-wide systems – Intranet, rotation of talent across functions and countries, temporary co-location of people, etc. – ensuring that you're not only a collection of intelligent nodes, but a collectively intelligent community?

## Can you get customers to work for you?

In relation to your customers, democratization of information is extremely good news if you know how deal with the situation in a smart way. These days, for many companies the biggest untapped asset is the pool of thousands of well-educated customers who are at least in theory willing to do pro bono work for them. The year 2007 marked the 40th anniversary of the ATM (automatic telling machine) (and the Big Mac). At the same point in time as the Beatles released the Sgt. Pepper's Lonely Hearts Club Band album, banks started to outsource parts of their operations to us. 40 years later, this opportunity is open to all companies. Believe it or not, a lot of people want to take a more active part in what you're currently doing for them. It's up to you to give them the right tools and incentives. What could your organization learn from Facebook and others with user generated content?

Real customization means providing a platform so that the customer can co-design and/or co-produce his or her own limited edition product, service or experience – not more variation. Dell came to dominate its industry by using a standardized interface enabling us to make a number of important design choices for a few basic PC models – manageable mass-customization. Production and consumption here merge into "prosumption," a term coined by futurist Alvin Toffler already back in 1980. Today, Australian beer company Brewtopia lets its customers design the product (beer, wine, water), packaging and promotion. A customized beer is yours for $2.29. More questions:

- How could you turn more of your consumers into prosumers?
- How will you enable and motivate them to do some of the things that you currently probably do in-house?
- Could you even charge (some of) them for doing part of your work?
- What are you going to do about it – tomorrow?

## Do you know the new rules of attraction?

When people have been liberated, they will make choices and move around – as consumers and competents – from organization to organization. Choice means search. This implies that you as a leader and your organization are players in a great global attraction game. You'll have to court them. Courtship begins with trying to figure out what makes them tick. We differ. Different things make us mad, sad and glad. Human beings aren't bulk goods. So, what you offer will have to differ. Personalize or perish.

Most companies have spent the last 20 years mass-customizing in relation to their consumers. During the upcoming 20 years clever companies will spend a lot of time and effort mass-customizing also the employee deal. Indeed, some have already done their homework. At the whacky and highly successful Brazilian company Semco, run by the maverick Ricardo Semler, there are more than 10 different ways to get paid – ranging from a fixed salary to stock options, royalties and bonus schemes, all of which can be combined in various ways. The company uses flextime. Employees evaluate their bosses. Semler has also established a profit-sharing system and insists that the financials are published internally, so that everyone can see how the firm is doing. At Semco, employee turnover is about 1%.

Everything can be personalized – anything from office furniture to incentives. Most companies know that. Some organizations are indeed doing things about it. At IBM and Sun Microsystems between 40 and 50% of the workforce already do their jobs remotely. But change is slow. Why do an absolute majority of all firms design compensation schemes only for those who live to work and not for the absolute majority of people who work to live? For many people, a couple of days at home with the kids when they have the flu can be worth a whole lot more than a nicer company car. Why do most corporations define excellence only for those at the top? Should a company where those who face the moment of truth on a daily basis have no standard against which to measure their greatness really expect to be that successful? Individualization is the key to effective people leadership. Case closed.

Not everything should be personalized, however. Winning the great global attraction game isn't only a question of full-blown flexibility. Firms also need to fix a number of things. If you try to be everything to everyone in the workforce, you'll probably not mean that much to anyone. If you're distinct in what you offer talent and tell them what you expect from them, your firm becomes self-selecting. Total flexibility means that everyone is a potential visitor, also those that you don't want hanging around. Standardization and personalization must co-exist.

People are tribal. Both talent and consumers will look for organizations that can provide them with meaning. If you're looking for buy in think bio. As noted earlier, an increasing number of competitive communities are biographical – made up of people who believe that they have something in common. The few things that are shared within the organizational tribe open up for diversity and variation.

- What's at the core of your tribal bible – the non-negotiables?
- Why should people work for you and shop from you?
- Who shouldn't join – is this clear to you *and* them?
- Would you hire yourself?
- Name three things that are already personalized, then come up with three more things that you're going to individualize during the next month.
- What three practical measures are you going to take to invite customers to join the tribe?

## Are you in touch with your feminine side?

Faith Popcorn, once dubbed the "Nostradamus of marketing" by *Fortune*, called one of her latest books *EVEolution*. The reason is quite obvious. When freedom is a little bit more evenly distributed between men and women, the latter group becomes more of a factor to consider. Our society is becoming increasingly feminized. Girl power! These days, even the villains are female; the 21st century gang of four foxes – Britney, Paris, Nicole and Lindsay (also referred to as the Cat Pack by *Details*). Bad girls abound while there's a genuine shortage of bad boys. As the *Daily Mail* recently put it; "Girls are the new boys."

This trend actually extends way beyond women becoming more powerful also in business. The most famous soccer player on our planet, David Beckham, is an interesting character. He is married to an ex-Spice Girl (well Posh is actually a true Spice again as the band has re-united). Occasionally, Becks walks around in a sarong. He waxes his chest. We don't know about you, but we have a really hard time imagining someone like Kaiser Franz Beckenbauer waxing his chest. Admit that there's something quiet fascinating about the fact that the most popular player in a traditional macho and working-class kind of sport is a so called metro sexual man.

Think Las Vegas. What comes to mind? Gambling? Strip-joints? Siegfried and Roy? What happens in Vegas stays in Vegas? Traditionally that used to be the case. Over time, however, entrepreneurs in Vegas began to realize that this focus really limited their growth potential – few families (possibly with the exception of the Bundy's from the TV-show *Married with Children*) and women will be that attracted by this particular combo. In effect, Sin City has changed. Now, you'll find an increasing number of spas, shows and shopping malls (right next to the strip-joints). And the great thing about the strategic re-orientation is that if you get the women, the guys will come anyway. We're not saying that this effort to re-energize Vegas will be successful – it has to be authentic – but it's still interesting to note the power of commerce over tradition.

Over and above anything else, EVEolution is of course about women becoming more of a force to be reckoned with also in the business world. Women know how to navigate in a socio-economic landscape that's intellectual, psychological and social – brain- rather than brawn-based. More opportunities = more money = more power. Now, that's hardly big news, but the sad truth is that far too many executives still suffer from thinking about women and treating women as if they were just small men – miniature replicas of the real thing. Nothing could be less true. Whatever you do – don't think pink and 6% smaller. Men and women are just different – very, very different. Ever struck you?

Martha Barletta has written some fantastic stuff on these differences and the difficulties involved in marketing to women with the traditional testosterone method. Let's begin with the basic stuff. Our senses differ. Consider just one; vision. Men have better focus, while the peripheral vision of women is superior. Why? Evolution – spelt the old-fashioned way this time. During the Stone Age, men went out hunting and you needed great focus to kill an animal. The women typically stayed home and took care of the kids and elderly. If someone was sneaking up trying to attack you, great peripheral vision was a plus. As Barbara and Allan Pease put it in *Why Men Don't Listen & Women Can't Read Maps*, "This is why modern men can find their way effortlessly to a distant pub, but can never find things in fridges, cupboards or drawers." Reflection time:

- Does your strategy sufficiently reflect the growing importance of feminization and the female gender?
- Does the composition of your leadership team sufficiently reflect the growing importance of feminization and the female gender?
- Does your leadership style sufficiently reflect the differences between men and women?
- Are your value propositions for employees and customers, respectively, hetero- or just homo-sexual?

It even turns out that men and women shop differently. Martha Barletta provides a telling example of "Jack and Jill." At the shopping mall, they are given the same mission; Go to Gap, and buy a pair of pants. Jack, the determined and focused prioritizer quickly solves the problem. After six minutes he has a pair of trousers that cost him $33. What about Jill, a representative of a gender somewhat more complicated, interested in maximizing, getting more info and the best deal possible? How much time? Three hours and 26 minutes! Jill did not go straight to the Gap, however. That wasn't the mission. She zigzagged between all the stores at the mall – Macy's, JC Penny, Sears, etc. Finally, she went to Gap and got the pants. How much money do you think she spent? Answer: $876!

So what does the behavior of Jack and Jill imply? Well, we've given it a lot of thought. This is our take on it. The example is the ultimate evidence that men spend more money per time unit than women when they go shopping – very efficient. Just do the math . . . But that conclusion sort of misses the somewhat greater point; that a lot of corporations are missing out on a mega opportunity when they persist in treating women as if women were just small men.

In our neck of the woods, an absolute majority of most important purchasing decisions are taken by women. Yet, only a minute minority of all products and services are designed by women for women. You don't need a PhD in business to realize that this is a mega-imperfection that sooner or later someone will begin to exploit. Right now, women happen to be the greatest business opportunity for just about any company in any industry in most parts of the world. Consider the Nobel Peace Prize Laurate Mohammad Yunnus. His Grameen Bank started by lending small sums of money to poor, peasant Bangladesh women.

Let's face it. Women are just much better equipped to deal with the complexities of today's world. By now, we have enough research to fill a decent-sized library suggesting that the characteristics we expect to find in leaders capable of re-energizing and successfully running a modern company are clearly overrepresented among women. Men may not be inefficient, but in the light of the current non-linear developments we could very well end up increasingly irrelevant. After all, we're already superfluous when it comes to breeding kids. And remember that irrelevance is a much greater problem than inefficiency. Dodo bird: 17th century. Dodo bloke: 21st century? Birds will rule!

## Economic freedom

More obvious than the effects of a deregulated life is the fact that a deregulated economy will have a direct impact on what it takes to be successful. For sure, the current wave of market mania increases the pressure on leaders. Yesterday's news? Then, keep in mind that in all likelihood we ain't seen nothing yet. Right now, a little more than one fifth of all world output is open to global competition. If you're to believe current research, in the not too distant future we're going to reach 80%. Unless there's a major trade war, the train to Marketville appears quite unstoppable. And when the economy is driven by variations in demand rather than one big master plan developed centrally, don't be surprised that we experience more surprise.

We believe there are three key reasons why we should expect this development to continue, or perhaps even pick up speed; those related to the role of information, institutions and identity, respectively. All of the reasons give rise to new questions that you need to think about when envisioning the future.

## Is information working for or against you?

At the end of the day, a market is just a big conversation – hundreds of sellers communicating with thousands of buyers trying to determine the price of something. Think bazaar. As an effect of the climate change, we've moved from an info desert to a veritable information jungle. So, hardly surprising markets flourish, because they feed and breed on info.

This puts an enormous pressure on firms to be absolutely world-class on everything that they do. Markets imply a choice; make it or buy it. The vertically integrated company that made everything internally and dominated business for about a century thus becomes an endangered species. Are you prepared to accept these consequences or are there still holy cows in your organization – business areas, functions, activities, etc. that are kept in-house for historical reasons? Markets are a lot of things but certainly not nostalgic.

## Could you take advantage of institutional changes?

Without doubt, many barriers of international trade have fallen during the last few decades. Since 1980, global GPD has grown at almost 6% annually, but international trade and capital flows have grown even faster. The world economy is bigger *and* increasingly globally connected.

Governments have been back-tracking and now the market is the dominant institution on our planet. The wisdom of crowds has replaced the plans constructed by the masters of social-engineering. Markets are merely self-organizing mechanisms – machines for sorting the efficient from the inefficient. Markets recognize efficiency, but it's also just about the only thing they are aware of. They are certainly not substitutes for responsibility. This leaves modern organizations with a moral dilemma; how can you pursue the new opportunities without being seen as an exploiter of those less fortunate – a responsible revolutionary?

## Can you be a supplier of identity?

Imagine that you're at a dinner party. You've been seated right next to a person whom you've never ever met before. What will be the first couple of questions – the ice breakers – that you'll ask this man or woman? Our experience is that "So, what do you do for a living?" and "Where do you come from?" end up on the top three list in most cultures. We ask these questions because we're trying to pin down the identity of the other person in order to increase the odds of being able to have an interesting discussion during the rest of the dinner.

You arrive at the dinner party with two working hypotheses; identity is shaped by production and location. History tells us that there should be statistically significant differences between construction workers and male hair-dressers, as well as between those born in India and Indiana, respectively. That used to be true, and perhaps to some extent it still is, but now also other factors are growing in importance. These days, there could be more of a difference between someone who's dressed in a Gucci suit and someone who always shops at H&M than between a person born in Budapest and another one who grew up Buenos Aires. Identity is increasingly shaped by consumption. Such "buyo-graphical" tribes are already here. People shop around for a unique(?) personality.

In most parts of the world, the church and the state are no longer the dominant providers of identity they once were. This leaves all organizations with a new challenge; how can you fill the vacuum that currently exists? To be a credible provider of personality you have to sell something more than mere products and services. Take some time off and do the following exercises:

- What's the persona of your customer offering?
- How are they and the experience you provide supposed to make your customers feel like celebrities?
- Write down the top five characteristics that capture the character, traits and qualities of what you have to offer – if you can't do it how are we – the consumers – supposed to be able to?
- Pick up a couple of magazines and make a collage of pictures that capture the identity you're trying to supply the market with. Are you

getting the message across with your current design and communications strategies?

## Upstairs and downstairs

Combine the deregulated life with a deregulated economy and the socio-economic landscape changes shape. In the 1970s a renowned German cosmetics company proclaimed that its strategy focused on making "products for average looking women." Ponder this. Have you ever met a woman, or a metro sexual man for that matter, who in the morning stands in front of the mirror and says; Today, I think I'm going for average. Yet, you can almost hear the leaders of this company talking about it. In the board (bored?) room of Cosmetics Gmbh, the chairman stands up and says:

> "As you know my friends, during the last few years, we have done extensive market research. I am proud to tell you that the results are conclusive; it turns out that most women look average. And since we want a larger share of the market we have decided to sell cosmetics to Average Looking Women!"

As ludicrous as this slogan may sound to the enlightened individualists of the 21st century, such a marketing mentality could dominate so long as demand exceeded supply and the business world was local and normal – with a flourishing middle-class, mass-markets, standardization, stability and dominated by any gender so long it was male. Yesterday, success was a question of appealing to the local average where the bulk of business could be found.

That was then. This is your now. **Forget about normal. Think abnormal.** Remember that markets sort stuff – products, people and corporations – based only on the principle of efficient or not. The overall effect of privatizing life and business is that we're currently on a journey that brings us into a world of economic Darwinism – a double economy where the gap between the best and the rest is increasing – a roller-coaster reality.

In this split society, some people have to take on double jobs just to scrape a living whereas another group of people – the group we suspect you belong to – work 60, 70, or perhaps even 85 hours per week; the staminacs. Why do we work so much? Let's give you a clue. What are your personal competitive advantages? You've probably not reached your current position by being extremely fast or strong (if Arnold picked up a copy of the book to further re-energize California, we apologize. After all, as the Arnold character in the *Simpsons* movie puts it – he was elected to lead, not to read). In all likelihood, you owe your success to smartness.

Congratulations, the nerds have won! People like you and we should be extremely happy that we were born right now. Think about the historical odds for being born at a point in time when brain beats brawn – minuscule. If people like us had been born during the middle-ages most of us would have been dead by now – well, we guess we would have been in any case, but at least before turning 30. Let's face it, there's not a lot of Gladiator material in your typical 21st century executive.

But we were lucky enough to be born at a point in time when you compete(d) on competence, smartness, knowledge – call it whatever you like. Yet, all of that soft stuff is a bit weird. As pointed out earlier, knowledge comes with a best before date. Unless you use it now there's a clear risk that tomorrow it will be obsolete and commercially worth-less. So, we work and work and work . . . No wonder that most of us find it increasingly difficult to strike that delicate balance between making a living and having a good life.

## In short supply

By now you may ask – and rightly so – why are these societal trends so important to think about. Most business books go straight to ten bankable propositions and then proceed by telling you how to make it. As pointed out in the beginning of this chapter, we're convinced that great entrepreneurial leaders have always been marvellous sociologists. In most industries, you can make money only on things that are placed in the intersection of what's scarce and in demand. Envisioning the future of a firm therefore requires that you develop hypotheses about how and in what respect consumer and employee reasoning and behavior changes as the greater social-economic landscape evolves.

What is and will be scarce differs from person to person, industry to industry, region to region. One of us is from Sweden, a country where a few years ago the consequences of change had led to a situation in which the top three bestselling prescribed pharmaceuticals were; Viagra, Prozac, and Losec (for ulcers). Apparently, in this part of the world people demand to be horny, happy and calm. We do believe, however, that there are some general principles to keep in mind when you discuss these matters at the office.

A while back we came across a fascinating Danish study of how a typical Dane spends a day – 24 hours. The original study had been conducted back in the early 1980s. Then, they decided to repeat it 20 years later. What would be your guess for the activity that had increased most, percentage wise, in terms of taking up time in an average Danish person's life? Rule out using a mobile phone and surfing the Web, things that were not commercially viable in the early 80s. Time spent . . . ? To our astonishment (at times, even we're surprised), we realized that it was time spent in the toilet. Why? Let's tell you why. In this globally interconnected, hypercompetitive, communications based and stressful world of ours, the toilet is one of the few places in which it's still legitimate to be alone.

These days, solitude (not loneliness which there is in abundance and may account for the consumption of Prozac and Losec), when you choose to be alone, is really scarce. So is silence, everything that's slow, open space, authenticity and risk-free tension. Our lives are pretty predictable and boring so to escape we play Grand Theft Auto on our game consuls. We kill without any risk of getting caught.

Does all this matter? Well, if you're IKEA, the Danish love for loos matters a lot. People are no longer spending as much money furnishing their living room because they are building Roman baths and spas. That has clear strategic implications. It matters a lot if you're an insurance company. Some 20 years ago, a claim for water damages may have been around 1000 euros. Today, that claim is likely to be in the area of 5000 or perhaps even 15 000 euros. Signal in on the scarce.

## Take the fitness and sexy test

Once you have an idea about how demand and the sentiment of people may change, you must focus your attention on figuring out how to exploit that opportunity. In our deregulated world, there are two basic options per opportunity. As mentioned in the beginning of the book, either you design a strategy that's as fit as the great white shark – well adapted to a world of markets, or you focus on being sexy like the peacock with his amazing tail – attractive to people with more or less endless choice. Most people are familiar with Charles Darwin's idea of survival of the fittest. As an effect of the deregulated business life and our journey into an info jungle where markets rule and reign also organizations must adapt. Right now, they are outsourcing and off-shoring to become the fittest business on the block.

Just farming out stuff won't do the trick, however. Being fit requires that you find and exploit a market imperfection. For economists (and politicians) perfect markets are those where marginal cost equals marginal revenue and companies make just enough money to stay in business. In a perfect market, profits don't exist. It's therefore the duty of executives to pursue imperfections.

Dell created a *transactional* advantage with its direct to the customer business model, eliminating several parts of the traditional value chain. eBay has designed its Internet platform, where you can sell and buy just about everything, in such a way that relationships and reputation evolve and result in mutual *trust*. Finally, there are those companies, mainly professional service firms such as Ernst & Young or Accenture, which focus their attention on creating and defending a *talent* monopoly.

But also Darwin later came to realize there's another way. The trick lies in shifting perspective from a survival-oriented to a courtship-based view of success. Consider the peacock's tail? From a fitness perspective, this "psychedelic feather duster" actually provides a competitive disadvantage. He can't run. He can't fly. So, why did the peacock end up with such a ridiculous costume?

In order to understand his look, we must consider the peahen, because in nature as in life and in business it's always the "customer" who takes the ultimate decision; go – no go. Why? It's really quite simple. Nature is practically organized. Given an unlimited supply of women, the average man could probably produce about 150 kids per month – if he only focused and that as you know by now, men are pretty darn good at. The average woman, on the other hand, even given an unlimited supply of exceptionally virile Brad Pitt clones, is somewhat more restricted to about one child per year. And given that, isn't it reasonable that women in general happen to be a little bit more picky, if you know what we mean?

When a peahen catches sight of a peacock this kick-starts a three-step process. Here's the executive summary.

Step 1: Wow, what a guy (he is a walking bill-board)!
Step 2: Is he alive, because he shouldn't be (not with that ridiculous costume)?
Step 3: If you can survive with such a flamboyant outfit; you must have some extra energy in the system; be really smart (it's not a good idea to be stupid if you look like a peacock); you must have really good . . . genes!

And the peahen goes crazy.

With the tail, the peacock is actually telling the female that he is so incredibly fit that he can afford to carry around this awkward adornment and still be alive and have a good life.

It took research 125 years to figure this out. In the 1970s, the Israeli researcher Amotz Zahavi proposed what he called the "theory of having a credible handicap." The greater the handicap, the more attractive you become – provided that you're alive. You become successful not despite, but thanks to the handicap. It sends out a signal; "hey, take a good look at me. As you can see I should be dead, but I'm not. Try to figure that one out if you can . . ." Already Darwin hinted some of these thoughts when he wrote about the importance of attraction, fertility and sexual selection.

You may be thinking that survival of the sexiest goes only for stupid animals, and not for human beings. Then you're dead wrong. Why do you think men play golf, collect sports cars and go off to the Himalayas to climb Mount Everest? What signals are guys who do such things sending to all the women of the world do you think? Well, if you can spend a lot of time on a lower form of agriculture, collect vehicles that are useless from a transportation point of view, and go off to Tibet twice a year while still keeping your job as an exec at a very successful international IT-company, then you must have . . . really good genes.

The human brain is our tail. From research in neuroscience we also know that the brain's limbic system, which governs our feelings, is much more powerful than the neocortex that controls intellect. The traffic instructions that evolution provided our brains with are pretty clear: emotions always have the right of way.

## Profiting from the peacock principle

Since we've deregulated life and moved into a split society in which at least some people now have more or less endless choice, being good is often no longer enough. Today, in the business world we find an abundance of firms that supply a surplus of products and services with similar quality, price and performance. For Generation Choice – sameness sucks. So, corporations must attract the attention of people by appealing to their feeling – exploit the inperfections of man.

In business, credible handicaps largely fall into two separate categories: *ethics* and *aesthetics*. If you refuse to bribe and cheat, you'll be handicapped. Corporate social responsibility costs = handicap. Also corporations that spend a lot of money on being environmentally friendly develop a handicap – a cost disadvantage. Is this handicap credible? Increasingly so, we believe, after the UN report on our climate and Al Gore's documentary *An Inconvenient Truth*. No wonder that the percentage of global venture capital that's invested in so called clean technology is up from 1% in 2000 to 14% in 2006. But ethics isn't for everyone, everywhere. All handicaps are subjective, and their exchange rates vary over time and space. As a supplier you also need to be authentic. Transparency works both ways.

As for aesthetical handicaps, consider BMW. We've been told that the company employs close to 30 highly trained engineers who work only on the sound of the door, and almost half as many who focus on the smell of the car. Look at the cost structure of that company. BMW shouldn't exist – not in one of the most competitive industries in the world; not when it spends an enormous amount of time and money on completely "meaningless" things such as design and branding. Yet, it does. In a perfectly normal and rational world we would all be driving Toyota Corollas. We don't. BMW is hugely successful – not despite the handicap but thanks to it. The company knows how to profit from the peacock principle.

# Creating the confidence clinic

**12**

## May the force be with you

People may own the most critical resource of today's economy, their own brain. But while mysteriously complex, it isn't only an intellectual tool. As we've seen, this little mushy mass of grey and white matter weighing some 1.3 kilograms is also our emotional center. So, why is the soft stuff so central in business where rational reasoning is supposed to rule?

Let's bring the issue down to its most basic level. First take a closer look at individual work-related performance. At your company, you probably have some colleagues who are above average performers. Others are abysmally below and some are just on par. This is more or less a statistical necessity (unless you ask a group of men because then everyone will swear that he is most definitely an above average performer). What then determines the differences between belonging to the top and being a flop?

In a world of competence-based competition it would seem logical to conclude that winning the race boils down to having and utilizing intellectual capital. Research shows that education and experience – the two major IC components – account for 28% of the variation we find in work-related performance. For a scholar these stats are close to Nirvana. But, it also turns out that one psychological factor alone explains 38% of this variation. That factor happens to be confidence – self-efficacy and self-belief. The belief in your own ability to generate the motivation and cognitive resources necessary to achieve your objectives actually seems more important than the ability as such. And this is just one psychological variable.

Today, psychological forces are at least as important as intellectual ones. This isn't the time and place to have a lengthy discussion about all the reasons behind this development. Suffice to say that the homogenization of articulate knowledge through increasingly standardized education has probably contributed to the decline of Nerdworld. All MBA students now know their Michael Porter and Philip Kotler by heart. And what everyone knows is usually not worth a great deal.

Psychological capital, on the other hand, can't be copied by your competitors – it's person specific. In addition, since the limbic system that governs our emotions runs on an open-loop, feelings are contagious, positive ones more so than negative. Boost the psychological capital of one employee and that person becomes an ambassador of positive energy spreading the good virus. Psychological development is a self-enforcing process. So long as you ignite the process others will carry the torch and help you re-energize the corporation. Start it up and sparks will fly.

Sony Europe is now embarking on a program of development for its most senior talents that focuses almost entirely on the emotional intelligence aspects of leadership. Sony's approach involves (among many other things) senior managers talking to water as it freezes and seeing how their tone of voice and emotions affect the formation of ice crystals – weird but interesting to see the effects of human emotions and mental states on things around you. You don't find unusual insights from looking in the same places as other people!

## Peak-performers

Talent is multifaceted and not restricted to raw IQ. So, the outcome of any process involving talent is dependent on more than one dimension. Look no further than yourself. Can you do the dishes? Probably. But do you love to do the dishes? Less likely. Would you love to be able to bend it like Beckham? Sure. Can you do it? No way (we doubt that Roberto Carlos reads business books).

This is what we're getting at. Most successful people who we know can answer two specific questions with only one answer. Those two questions are: a) What do you do for a living?, and b) What do you love most in life?

"The artist is nothing without the gift, but the gift is nothing without work," Emile Zola remarked. Peak performance requires that we create conditions where people can focus on doing things where they can combine skill with will – proficiency and passion – learning the tricks of the trade and loving what you do. Getting one out of two right will not get you to the top.

**Skill**

|  | Low | High |
|---|---|---|
| **High** | Fiery-spirit | Peak-performer |
| **Low** | Play-worker | Brainy-drainer |

(Will)

Skill and will largely correspond to what American academic Steve Kerr and his colleagues call "substitutes for leadership." Imagine that you're in charge of an organization where each and every person has high skill and will in relation to all their tasks. Under these circumstances you wouldn't be needed. But as soon as there's a drop in one of these dimensions you must step in and support that individual or team. Be careful, however. If people lack in will and you read the situation as one characterized by a skill shortage, or vice versa, they will probably rebel when you take action.

## Highs and flows

Take a moment to think about one of the best work experiences you've had, something that made you feel proud when you finished it. What did it feel like in terms of energy? Did you get a buzz out of achieving something that was challenging and worthwhile?

We suspect few of you reflected on the recent implementation of a new policy on car hire or the disposal of waste, important though that work might have been. We guess that many of the images that came to mind were of you completing something that was important but difficult, that engaged you fully, something that meant working hard and close with colleagues and peers, but also something that made you feel as though you made a difference.

These high energy, high workload, high achievement times are what Mihaly Csikzentmihalyi (possibly the toughest surname in the world to spell) calls *flow states*. These are times when the match of challenge and will/skill sets seems to magically meet. It's when to get things done we call on all of our unique abilities. In these experiences time distorts, either passing quickly as the person is so immersed in the work, or passing very slowly allowing all aspects to be considered in detail without pressure.

In times of flow people are completely absorbed and fulfilled. This can happen to individuals many times a day in those that have roles closely aligned with their personal skill sets and attitudes. The poor souls trapped in roles not suited to them, yet still asked to perform miracles in the business, rarely experience the joy of being absorbed in something meaningful. Their personal reaction is more often stress and anxiety which breeds fear and withdrawal. This isn't a recipe for success.

Maybe we can't lead people into states of flow all the time, but by knowing more about individual needs, matching these as much as possible to the needs of the organization, the leader can create more opportunities for people to experience flow-like work. People work better, with more ideas, increased creativity, more energy and higher output when they are happy!

## Positive psychology

As soon as you initiate a discussion including the words psychology, psychologist or therapy, most executives become defensive and conclude their remarks by saying something like: "I'm not insane – so there's no need for that mumbo jumbo, touchy-feely kind of stuff, thank you." Soul-searching may not be macho, but we promise that it will become an absolute necessity if you want to make mucho. After all, the question of what constitutes "the good life" has been with us since the times of Plato, Socrates and Aristotle. Beyond the initial and emotional testosterone reaction, there are also some more rational reasons why executives have been skeptical about the business value of psychology.

During the latter part of the 20th century, the field of psychology was by and large focused on addressing mental illness rather than mental wellness – William James' work on "healthy mindedness" at the turn of the previous century and Maslow's work on humanistic psychology during the 1950s and 60s provide two notable exceptions. With this disease model of human functioning in mind, also psychologists tried to turn minuses into zeros. For many years, psychology had rather little to say about what makes (business) life worth living.

There was a logical rationale behind this. After WWII, for natural reasons, there was a lot of work related to treating mental illness. The market for shrinks was growing. Compassion is also alluring. Those who are suffering should be the first to be helped.

In the pre-war period, however, in addition to curing mental illness, psychology also included research focused on making our lives more productive and fulfilling, as well as studies centered on identifying and nurturing talent. This line of more proactive work became mummified in the post-war years.

More recently, a new movement in psychology has begun to take up the study of these ancient questions: *positive psychology*. Spearheaded by people such as Martin Seligman and Mihaly Csikzentmihalyi, positive psychology is the study of "the strengths and virtues that enable individuals and communities to thrive."

Many influential thinkers in the field distinguish between three overlapping states of plus:

- **Pleasant Life** work, sometimes also referred to as "life of enjoyment," focuses on positive experiences. It captures the important dimension of *time* – how we relate to experiences of the past, present and possible futures.
- The second line of work concerns the **Good Life** ("life of engagement") and shifts focus from time to individual *traits* – having a positive personality – using our strengths and virtues.
- The final plus area of interest is the inquiry into the **Meaningful Life** or "life of affiliation". Here, issues looked upon concern in what types of institutional contexts people flourish – the *tribal* dimension.

Growing the psychological capital by re-energizing your organization therefore requires a focus on both the individual and the institutional environment, and the interplay between the two over time. What really matters is in one word: relationships.

Recently, business scholars have started to apply some of the ideas present in the positive psychology movement. We've found a framework developed by American academics Fred Luthans and Carolyn Youssef very valuable when talking to executives about why it's so critically important to actively deal with the psychological dimension of re-energizing individuals and teams. Their model focuses on four variables that are state-like, rather than dispositional, and that all have a scientifically proven positive impact on performance: confidence, hope, optimism and resiliency. Since the variables aren't fixed, they can be developed. And at most organizations, according to our experience, there's a lot of room for improvement. Based on the work of Luthans and Youssef, let's see just how you can contribute to constructing a clinic that makes commercial sense.

## Kings of confidence

Confident people always seem go for the toughest tasks, have a fantastic ability to tap into that final percent of motivation, and just appear to keep on trying when faced with difficulties. Everyone may not be able to boast the confidence of someone like Mohammad Ali, proclaiming themselves "king of the world," but we can all improve. In addition to the obvious importance of positive feedback, there are several other ways in which you can boost self-efficacy and self-belief.

We all know that success breeds confidence. But in order for people to experience true success there must first be clear and measurable goals – not only for those at the top. These need to be goals that are challenging yet achievable – so called stretch-goals. Re-energizing leaders coach people and help them in the process of breaking down larger tasks into subtasks and sequence events so that there's a great probability of success in the initial stages. Then, they don't hesitate to celebrate small wins and early victories.

To energize your colleagues, you can also simulate success. You wouldn't put a fresh pilot straight into a Boeing 747, but these people still need to grow their self-belief by experiencing success. In response to this dilemma, we've invented pilot flight training. Invent you own simulators, use business games or just team up your young turks with the best leaders of your organization so that they can learn from and piggy-back on their success. Magnificent mentors do provide the so far only mediocre with a model for how to act, lead and succeed. The Pygmalion effect increases performance.

## Optimism Inc.

Optimism is all about what we attribute success and failure to. Optimistic people believe that good things are due to internal, permanent and omnipresent causes or conditions, whereas their explanations for bad things are attributed to external, temporary and more situation-specific circumstances. In short, they are convinced that success mostly happens by choice whereas failure generally comes about by chance. This explanatory style boosts their morale and self-esteem. Perpetual optimism is what former US Secretary of State General Colin Powell once called a "force multiplier." Note, however, that we're talking about the need for developing a realistic and flexible kind of optimism, not a Polly-Anna view of the world where everything is rosy red and people are prepared to take enormous risks and act irresponsibly.

Research suggests that energizing people by boosting optimism boils down to helping them come to terms with experiential issues related to the dimension of time. For people to have a positive outlook on life, you must first aid them in dealing with negative experiences from their past. Re-energizing leaders convince colleagues that historical failures are just necessary learning experiences – investments rather than costs. They persuade people to forgive themselves for mistakes that they can no longer do anything to correct.

There's a well-known legend about how one of IBM's most influential leaders, Thomas J. Watson Snr., had a meeting with a top salesperson who had recently lost $5 million on a project he had been working on. The guy was expecting to be fired. However, once he got into Watson's office, he was astonished to realize that Watson gladly started talking about the next big project they were planning. Bewildered, the salesman asked his boss if he was not going to fire him for the multi-million dollar loss. "Fire you?" replied Watson. "Why would we want to fire you when we've just spent $5 million training you?"

Optimism also grows when you can get individuals to appreciate the present. Help a person to feel content and thankful about everything that's good right now. Optimists enjoy the good stuff more than they feel anxious about all the bad things that happen. Many of us take a lot of positive things for granted until they are taken away. Leaders re-energize people by celebrating their pluses while they are still there. Finally, the greatest leaders also assist people in looking for future opportunities.

## Hope for the future

Napoleon once said: "A leader is a dealer in hope." Academics argue that how hopeful we are is dependant on the interaction between three variables: goals, agency and pathways. In general, hope rises when our goals seem urgent and we feel in control of the situation by sensing that we have the capability to influence things. Only then can we develop the capacity to come up with new ways to get around or solve problems in case our initial hunches about what to do did not help us in achieving our goals.

Strategies for re-energizing hope concern all three variables. Just as for developing confidence, goal-setting and communication of goals are critical in providing people with clear targets. Such goals leave us with the feeling that we can actually influence our destiny and develop different courses of action. Possessing the ability to re-target, and knowing when to change, also helps in avoiding false hope. From a leadership point of view, agency development is often contingent on delegation of some of your authority and on showing that you're confident in their ability to deal with the new responsibilities. Tell people that they will make it and more of them will.

Finally, the ability to develop multiple pathways is greatly enhanced by practicing. It's really quite simple. Like in sports, music and the theatre, the more you practice, the luckier you get. As Mark Twain put it: "It usually takes me more than three weeks to prepare a good impromptu speech". People, and organizations as diverse as the army and Shell, develop anticipatory capabilities by utilizing scenario- or contingency planning. This kind of training provides them with a superior ability to deal with whatever the world throws at them.

## Rubber ball resiliency

Re-energizing resiliency concerns your ability to help people bounce back after both negative and positive surprises.

A few years ago, our friend Manfred Kets De Vries wrote a very interesting piece in the *Harvard Business Review* talking about the dangers of feeling like a fake – an *imaginary ignorant*. The business world is inhabited not only by Neanderthal managers who are utterly convinced that they are God's finest gift to mankind. There's a surplus of unfortunate souls who are indeed very knowledgeable but also incredibly insecure. Such people have great difficulties coping with their own success. These are executives who believe that eventually (and every day you enter the office this day comes closer) someone is going to call their bluff – show the world that the emperor is indeed naked – by exposing their fantasy foolishness.

Not all execs belong to one of these two extreme groups, however. Academic studies suggest that some people have an uncanny ability to deal with surprise, setbacks and difficulties, and then bounce back to an even higher level. These individuals accept reality for what it is, strongly believe that life is meaningful and excel at improvising – realistic, faithful, inventors. As Nelson Mandela once put it: "The greatest glory in living lies not in never falling, but in rising every time we fall".

To energize resiliency research suggests we need to provide people with a floor, an elevator, and an engine. The floor, or safety-net, reduces the risk of negative outcomes. Think healthcare benefits, wellness programs, employment security or safety regulations. The elevator is there to increase the probability of positive outcomes. Firms that take the development of human resources seriously (and studies show that far too few do – not the most successful ones, however), allocate adequate resources, and focus on furthering the psychological capital of employees end up with people who are better equipped to deal with temporary setbacks. No magic here – just a simple fact of business life.

The engine helps people mobilize the power to adapt and deal with surprise by utilizing their assets – as an individual and an organization. For instance, so called learning organizations are much quicker than rigid bureaucracies in adapting to new realities. The overall organizational architecture therefore plays a pivotal role in enabling people to (or preventing them from) dealing with change.

# Composing the courage cathedral

**13**

## Your corporate religion

The greatest leaders in the world know a lot about the missing link. A diverse intellectual capital helps us to creatively envision the future and develop new ideas and strategies. To engage people we need to build a dynamic psychological capital. But unless we complement this with discipline in the form of a solid social-capital, we won't be able to effectively execute our strategies. "Everyone has talent", says author Erica Jong. "What is rare is the courage to follow that talent to the dark places where it leads."

Our experience is that people can be extraordinarily courageous and committed only when we have something to hang on to. We all want something to believe in. Without faith – no future. To experience that spark of energy, we need a sense of purpose. In fact, great leaders always serve an even greater purpose. During his inauguration speech in 1994, Nelson Mandela said: "I'm here not to lead, but to serve."

We often urge leaders to learn from the best rather than the closest. As for faith-based systems, consider the world's religions. They have social capital of a magnitude that not even Fort Knox could hold. It doesn't matter whether we're talking about Christianity, Islam, Buddhism, Hinduism, Judaism or whatever. They have been around for hundreds or in some cases even thousands of years, so they must be doing something right. Occasionally, the test of time matters.

You may think your company is all about managing and marketing intangibles. Well, religious organizations are selling products and services that no one has ever seen, at least not with any real level of statistical significance since Moses caught sight of the burning bush. At the risk of sounding blasphemous, believing in higher powers is a bit like going to the hairdresser – you don't know anything about the actual service until it may be too late, and the end-result may be purgatory or sheer oblivion, rather than just a bad hairdo.

According to the British-American Professor of religious history, Ninian Smart, all world religions, or world views, can be described using seven sacred dimensions of strategic spirituality:

- Ideological – Our Dream
- Mythical – Our Stories
- Ritual – Our Ceremonies
- Ethical – Our Values
- Emotional – Our Experience
- Material – Our Things
- Organizational – Our Structures

In our work with companies we've adopted and adapted this framework to business in order to re-vitalize the spirit of the organization and build a foundation for tapping into its social capital. The seven dimensions capture the institutional context that either enables or hinders you in the effort to re-energize the firm. Think of them as seven strings on a guitar. While the quality of the individual strings is critical, at the end of the day success will depend more on your ability to play great tunes. The different elements of your corporate religion must be aligned to support and reinforce one another. Tune your organization.

A corporate religion is similar to but also in some respects quite different from a corporate culture. While cultures are popularly defined as "the way we do things around here," your corporate religion also depicts "the why we do things together around here." A culture each and every organization has – just take a look at yourself in the mirror tomorrow morning if you don't believe us – a corporate religion is conceived, created and must therefore be nurtured. Cultures exist. Real corporate religions live and have a life.

# Dream on

All religions, secular and non-secular, are set in motion by an ideological dimension – there's a dream. And it's important that it *is* exactly a dream. As someone once suggested to us, there was probably a good reason for why Reverend Martin Luther King Jr. once proclaimed "I have a dream," and why at some point in time he decided not say "I have a five year plan"! Dreams are inspirational and lift us up where we belong.

Think about Christianity. Without the notions of life after death and Jesus sacrificing his life on the cross to abolish the sins of man, this religion would never have survived the catacombs of the Coliseum in Rome, let alone would it have conquered the world. Ultimately, this daring dream is all about re-creating heaven on earth. Think about business. Nokia dreams of a world where everyone is connected. Bill Gates dreamt about a PC on every desk in every home. Dreams give rise to temporary monopolies. Profits are merely by-products.

Dreams are important because they facilitate fusion enabling energy creation. Diversity of people and ideas, which is so critical for strategic innovation and corporate renewal to occur, make up the potential for either powder keg or melting pot. By having a shared dream, we increase the probability that the end result is melting pot rather than a big explosion.

Consider the United States of America. Here, we find extreme diversity, and most certainly from an economic perspective it has been incredibly successful – the powerhouse of the world economy. The US isn't a nation state or country in the traditional sense, however. Rather, the United States is a big, hairy, audacious idea – BHAI – just like Israel is an idea called Zionism. Also Dubai is increasingly a BHAI. It's currently the 224th largest city in the world, but ranks as number one in terms of construction cranes per capita. Dubai is adding enough office space to supply a major European city – every year. Or consider communist USSR – a big, hairy, audacious, *bad* idea, but still an idea.

The fact that the United States is an idea is interesting, because it means that each and every one of us who isn't already American can become American. We know that this is a ghastly thought for some, but it's still a fact of life. The US is a movement – a club – you can join it. We can choose to be American. How long do you think it takes to become Swedish? About 243 years – if you're born in Denmark. French or Japanese? Short answer: don't even think about it. But we can all become Americans. Even if you're born in Thal, Austria, by the time you turn 21 you can move to the US, become Mr Olympia, a D-actor, a C-actor, a B-actor, and then the Governor of California. You know who we're thinking about – Arnold. The US just mops up most of the talent on our planet – including footballers who wax their chest.

But since some people can love the idea called the US, others can of course hate it. The natural law of big ideas; you can be for or against them – it's a love or loathe situation. We've found it a little bit more difficult to find a couple of friends who Friday evening gather to share a few bottles of red wine and end up having an extremely heated debate on the topic of . . . Belgium! Great ideas attract and repel, but never leave us indifferent. If you want to say yes to a certain group of talent or customers you must also be distinct enough in your dream for this to imply a strong NO to others. To be meaningful, plus needs minus.

Dreams that provide people with meaning are rooted in the past, but aimed at the future. As the old saying goes, "if you don't have a sense of where you come from, going backward looks like progress". Therefore, the first step in the process of re-energizing by strengthening your social capital means revisiting and re-creating the BHAI. BP did it. The firm embarked on journey from British Petroleum to Beyond Petroleum. And if a 100 year old oil company can do it, so can you.

## Tall stories

We find a mythical or narrative dimension in all competitive communities – the stories that we create, spread, listen to, and take to our hearts. Tall tales make the dream come alive. Since people remember things narratively rather than paradigmatically, these stories also ensure that the ideology isn't forgotten. Legends and lore make things tangible and memorable. As noted by the authors of the *Cluetrain Manifesto* "Stories differ from information in that they have a start and a finish; they talk about events; not conditions; they imply a deep relationship among the events; stories are about particular humans; and stories are told in a human voice. As markets once again become conversations, marketers need to excel at telling compelling stories." Stories help us make sense of a world that at times seems quite senseless.

As noted earlier, contemporary companies do business in a veritable information jungle caused by the recent developments in the fields of telecommunications and IT. In an age where more and more power rests with global media and so called Netizens – the people who invade and inhabit the Web – stories about you and your firm will spread whether you like it or not. Remember the 40 000 new blogs that are added every day. The relevant questions therefore become those of what stories – the message, the meaning, and the media – and who's responsible.

At your firm, do you have a CSO – Chief Storytelling Officer? In fact, these days, everyone who currently works and all those who have ever worked for your organization has CSO tattooed on their foreheads. Are the stories these people tell seductive enough to attract talent and new consumers? Do they really boost the confidence, hope and optimism of your people? And in what ways can they help these individuals to bounce back once they have encountered difficulties or run into problems? What about the impact of heroes and villains – role-models and common enemies – in propelling the re-energizing process?

Research indicates that great stories generally follow a particular logic. From the point of view of the listener the following three principles appear to be key if you want to make the connection:

- **Give me a simple slogan:** Don't complicate things. Nike just wants to do it and Apple makes computers for the rest of us. Most people can't deal with info overload. British journalist Christopher Booker talks about the seven basic plots in his marvellous book with that very title. Pick one of them per story.
- **Give me some space:** Leave some room for the imagination of the listener. Good stories are prosumption oriented. Involvement means attachment. That's probably why the book is usually better than the movie.
- **Give me some more lovin**: Great storytellers are passionate and hypnotic – think Steve – Jobs and Balmer. The words are only part of the message. Practice the entire package – voice, look, rhetoric, and body-language.

IBM, for instance, prepares its leaders on how to get the right kind of stories to tell and re-tell by using a systematic nine step process:

1. Which stories do you like the best? The worst? Why?
2. Would you consider these real stories? Or are they story fragments? Anecdotes? Why?

3. Do any of these stories make you think of other stories you could contribute? Which ones? Why?
4. Do any of these stories make you want to comment on them or start a discussion on a topic that they raise? Which ones? Why?
5. How would you want these stories to be organized? Why?
6. If you were looking for a particular one of these stories, how do you think would be the best way to find it?
7. Do you think that some of these stories are appropriate for business and others aren't – or do you think they all are? What criteria would you use to decide if a particular story would be of use?
8. If you had a story to add to this list, how would you want to do it? By filling out a form? By being interviewed? By having a story-collector sit in on a group in which you told stories? By having a member of the group collect stories? How else?
9. If you had a story to add to this list, who would you want to read it? How much control would you like to have over who could read it?

Stories also serve the purpose of providing people with a shared language and definitions that open up for fusion of knowledge and less friction in the communication process. Self-organization is heavily dependent on people sharing an understanding of this basic building block in the idea-based corporation. Unless people can speak to one another and share knowledge, the organization is doomed to have merely pockets of individual creativity. A shared language is a necessary but not sufficient condition for such innovative group-processes to take place.

# Corporate celebration

The third dimension of a corporate religion is the ritual one – our ceremonies. Companies with an ability to re-energize their troops don't hesitate to celebrate their victories and memorable moments. American academics and consultants Terence Deal and M.K. Key have written a great book called *Corporate Celebration*. The authors argue that celebrations fill business life with both purpose and passion. Rituals serve the dual objectives of reattaching us to our roots, and helping us in realizing future dreams.

Their research suggests that rituals and ceremonies can play a pivotal role within modern corporations in dealing with a variety of issues such as recognition, triumphs, tragedies, transitions, product launches, training, etc. This dimension of corporate life, they claim, is fundamental, not frivolous, and must be given the same level of attention as other important business functions. Without ceremonies it's difficult to maintain, reinforce and transform your corporate religion. Rituals also carry the bonus advantage of giving rise to many of the stories that we mentioned earlier.

CEOs can be MOCs – Masters of Ceremonies. For more than 30 years, Nestlé's Rive-Reine International Training Center has brought together managers from around the world to learn from senior Nestlé managers and from each other. At least once a month, the CEO goes there to teach and listen. This has created an international network of managers based on shared experiences and a common corporate religion.

What do you celebrate? Who do you celebrate? When do you celebrate? What's the equivalent of Independence Day or July 14th at your firm? Perhaps you miss them? In the future, you'll most certainly need them. Our experience is that particularly European firms have a lot to learn from the best North American and Asian organizations when it comes to using rituals to unite the troops or celebrate individual achievements.

## Value your values

Tightly linked to the stories and ceremonies are the ethical aspects of the corporate religion – our values; the moral code of the organization. This dimension is more important now than ever. As we've pointed out, the business world of the information jungle is increasingly transparent. Right next to the "Hall of Fame," we find the "Hall of Shame." If you can't find the way, just ask Martha Stewart or the Enron/Andersen crowd for directions. Unless you're ET, information, and the flows of information, can't be controlled. We live, work, and have to do business in a Striptease Society.

Recent studies indicate that CEOs believe that the five most important corporate ethics issues facing the business community are: 1) regaining the public trust; 2) effective company management in the context of today's investor expectations; 3) ensuring the integrity of financial reporting; 4) fairness of executive compensation; and 5) ethical role-modeling of senior management. They all boil down to the character, courage and confidence of people inside your organization – especially those at the top.

When one of us was responsible for hiring high potential graduates in the mid 1990s the most important thing they looked for in the employer was a great development program. This was No. 1 in their decision criteria for accepting an offer. Today, that same independent source of research data has employer reputation and ethics as the No.

1 decision criteria. So the money starved recent graduate, often with large debts, is placing ethics and reputation above cash – interesting signal.

More and more so, modern companies realize that in order to avoid scandals and promote cooperation they will need to hire people for attitude and then train them for skill. A number of prima donnas don't make up an ensemble until they are willing to sing the same song. Increasingly, what binds us together and enables cooperation is values-based, rather than merely value-based. Shared values equal trust. And your values must be shared, otherwise they are operationally impotent.

We also know that values can't be invented; only (re-)discovered. If you want to change the values of your organization, you first have to exchange some of your people. To re-energize, values must reflect reality rather than be a case of wishful thinking. Therefore, it's usually a good idea to involve the entire organization in the re-discovery process. A couple of years ago, IBM did just that. For 72 hours top-management invited all 319 000 IBMers to take part in an open "values jam" on their global intranet. People showed up by the tens of thousands. IBMs Sam Palmisano claims that he was struck by how thoughtful and passionate people seemed about the company they choose to be a part of, but also admits that at times they were brutally honest. Grass-roots development may be time-consuming but makes engagement and execution so much easier.

Re-energizing the ethical dimension of your business means linking trust to three critical things;

- your organizational purpose
- your processes
- your top-people

Research suggests that strategic trust follows when employees buy into the dream. Your task is to convince them with communication. Organizational trust boils down to your systems, procedures and processes being consistent over time and space. Change requires some stability; otherwise the result is just chaos. Personal trust is a question of character, which from your point of view means showing your commitment to the religion in action – day, after day, after day, even when it means saying no to a deal or losing some short-term revenues.

Reputation, it's said, arrives on foot but leaves on horseback. Creating the values-based firm isn't a quick fix, but it will prove worthwhile in the long-term. And these days ethics isn't only an internal issue.

Tomorrow's customers will not settle for great value alone, they will also want values. Given the choice, few people are prepared to shop from toxic companies. Money and meaning will go hand in hand.

## Are you experienced?

The fifth dimension of a corporate religion concerns emotions – the experience your organization is trying to provide people with. What does your firm look like, feel like, taste like, smell like, sound like? What about the customer experience? Even a cool company such at Harley Davidson admits that at the end of the day, what it truly sells is "the ability for a 43-year old accountant to dress in black leather, ride through small towns and have people be afraid of him."

Most people have intense emotions about their work, company and bosses – and right now in far too many companies that emotion is dreadfully negative. Talent who dislike the experience you provide them with will either leave or, perhaps even worse, hang around and just pretend to work. As someone once put it; first they get dumbed down and then numbed out – dazed and confused. No matter what, in these organizations, both the costs and the number of lost opportunities are enormous.

Imagine the positive results you could attain if you had access to the personal best outputs of more of the people more of the time? Working with a full team of winners, people who give their personal best at work, is something to strive toward. To help corporations succeed in building an OWW4 – an organization worth working for – we sometimes ask execs to think about the following things in designing the ideal work experience.

- When, in the morning, people enter the office or factory floor, do they describe it as the "house of horrors" or "house of laughs"?
- Do people feel competent, confident, courageous and in control of their work and work experience?
- Is the word fun included in your mission statement?
- What basic emotional state do you want to invoke in your people during the different phases they go through when they are supposed to perform?
- What sense of self-esteem is involved in the experience?
- Are your people convinced that they are in a position to make valuable contributions to the success of your business?
- Do employees feel their efforts are properly recognized and rewarded?

Studies indicate that emotional distress has a negative effect on intellectual functioning. When employees feel stressed, their thinking becomes increasingly rigid and bereft of creativity. Research also shows that stress may cause biochemical, psychological, and neurological changes that hold back an individual's ability to take notice of and identify with other person's feelings. Therefore, the psychological, neurological, and physiological responses that shelter us from emotional pain also make us less intelligent. Experiences affect the enterprise.

## Things that really matter

All religions have a material or artistic dimension: our stuff; objects and things. The crucifix, for example, is still the most well-known brand symbol or logo in the world. Are your buildings, offices, products, etc. aligned to the other elements of the corporate religion? An organization that proclaims to be unique, innovative and different, can't with any remaining credibility force its employees to work in "Dilbert-land." Where do your people go to seek inspiration? What's the river Ganges, Mecca, Mount Fuji or St Peter's Church of your organization? What famous artist would you have paint your religion – Damien Hirst or Jan Vermeer?

We manage our structures, strategies and systems – why not also our space? Many companies are in great need of a new physical architecture. Traditional office buildings were designed for administration rather than innovation. In an era where we're heavily reliant on combination, cubicles just divide. Instead of using a space where people can hide and play work, the time has come to start thinking about what it would take to design a place enabling talent to play at work.

As noted by consultant and speaker Alexander Kjerulf it's a whole lot easier to be productive, creative and happy at work in a colorful, organic and playful environment than in a grey, linear and boring one. (By the way, check out his 12 ways to pimp your office on the web.) On his travels beyond Dilbert-land, Alexander has found a number of contemporary companies that are doing some pretty funky spatial experiments. At Pixar, the company that gave us *The Incredibles* and *Finding Nemo*, some of the people work in small huts that have been put into the office. At Red Bull's office in London there's a slide that people can use to go between floors. Mindlab is a meeting facility that's available to all employees at the Ministry of Economic and Business Affairs in Copenhagen. The heart of it is an egg-shaped meeting room. Inside, all the walls are whiteboards. You can write on any surface in there.

Take some time off and time travel. Go to the new MIT campus in Boston designed by architect Frank Gehry, a man who has seen the future.

## The trinity of structures

Finally, there's the institutional or structural dimension of your organization and the logic behind it. Just compare the highly centralized structure of the Catholic Church to the more decentralized nature of Protestantism. But considering only this dimension renders a far too simplistic view of corporate structures. Let's borrow another concept from Jonas's old friend and mentor Gunnar Hedlund. In reality, he claimed, all organizations contain three different types of structures; those of titles, talent and tasks, respectively. Think about one of your colleagues. Within the organization, this person is someone, knows something and does certain things. To understand the true nature of his or her work all aspects are important to grasp.

For a long time, the three structures overlapped in a way that meant that the positional structure of titles was a reasonable proxy also of what people knew and did. No more. In most companies, and particularly those that are high on knowledge intensity and extensity, senior executives no longer necessarily know more than people located elsewhere in the organization. At a certain point in time, someone like Henry Ford did (or at least thought he did). Do you think Nokia's President and CEO Olli-Pekka Kallasvuo can design or assemble one of its latest E90 phones?

The work that we do in creative processes often requires us to cooperate horizontally across the organization, rather than to send orders down a vertical chain of command to get things done. Mostly, it's someone else than the CEO of the firm who's in charge. In some cases these processes even involve people who sit outside the firm – suppliers and customers. On occasion, these people may lead the effort.

In effect, the three structures are drifting apart. Title ≠ Talent ≠ Task. Those organizations that try to hang on to the illusion that all this new complexity can be crammed into a three-dimensional or even four-dimensional matrix organization are bound to fail. Many nervous breakdowns are around the corner.

Re-energizing your organizational dimension means accepting complexity. Left to dominate, each of the three basic structures that we find in all corporations will result in a particular archetypal organizational form. Letting the titles of the positional system dominate will produce a traditional bureaucracy used for the exploitation of givens. If talent is the only organizing principle, we're left with a meritocracy. Finally, if tasks that we perform in processes drive the entire system the design resembles an adhocracy, just like in the case of the pure creator. All of these organizing models have their pros and cons. Resolving the paradox means combining the best of the three worlds. Your challenge is therefore to manage them all, simultaneously.

When envisioning the future, engaging your people, and executing new strategies, you'll have to rely on talent, your own and that of your colleagues and business partners. At times, to acquire resources and swiftly move from task to task, you'll have to rely on the formal authority vested in your own title and those of more senior executives whom you've formed alliances with. Always, be aware of the three structural dimensions. Constantly beware of relying only on one of them.

# PART TWO: HOW
## Energizing Action

# 14 The Es in energize

## The model

There are three Es in energize: Envision, Engage and Execute. They lie at the heart of our model of how to re-energize your organization.

The $3^e$ model is captured in three dimensions on the next page. Before we go any further, a caveat: In the Monty Python classic *Holy Grail*, an English knight sees the fabled castle of Camelot emerge in the distance. "It's only a model", he says, bringing people back to reality. The same thing applies in this case. The $3^e$ model has worked in a wide variety of situations for us. But, it isn't *the* truth. It's not the absolute silver bullet. It's not magic.

The $3^e$ model is based on practical experience, activities and approaches. If you treat the model as a collection of interlinked principles then you can apply them in almost any leadership or change situation with great results.

Read the diagram from left to right and top to bottom. It works in both dimensions depending on which area you're focusing on. From left to right you have the three core processes, *Envision*, *Engage* and *Execute*. From top to bottom you have the three elements of re-energizing, *Attributes*, *Attention* and *Actions*.

The nine boxes are shared by both a process and an element – so *Confidence* is part of what it takes to *Engage* but also an *Attribute*.

You'll realize as we go through the examples and the cases how this layout helps us think about not only why leadership is different but also how leaders make change happen.

We'll use this diagram as a tool to explain our examples. The diagram will be shaded to represent different levels of performance in each box. The darker the shading of the box the more of a concern this element of leadership is. The lighter the shading the better this aspect of leadership is demonstrated. As you read the rest of the section we'll illustrate our ideas with examples of people, real people in real situations and their profiles. We will draw from our experience of working with them, the strengths they applied and the areas of weakness as shown by the model. More crucially we'll explore the organizational implications of their leadership.

The people in the book are all known personally to us. We're pretty sure that when reading their profiles they could guess that we're talking about them. So, in many cases we've disguised their names to protect the innocent and not so innocent.

It is worth highlighting that there are three constants not featured in the model, but still critically important: creativity, communication and change. To be absolutely clear, these are aspects of all core processes. You can be creative in how you envision, engage and execute. The same is true as for the necessity of effective communication throughout the entire change process. Change is therefore not an output, but a throughput in our model.

The three Es have a natural progression from envisioning onwards. Leaders should direct their energy to each at different points. The model shows a movement from top left to bottom right, from using their competence to building capability. Occasionally, there may be times when you could be forced to go back and re-envision or re-engage. What follows is the route through that maze, a guide to successfully navigating the model and making change happen.

# 15  Envision

## We can see clearly now

Envisioning is the process of creating clarity about what's possible, what's necessary, and why this is so. It's not easy to get excited about the business you're working in if you don't know where it's going. This isn't just a question of lacking commitment, but a basic human need to know *why* we're doing something. Creating that shared picture of the future requires leadership. Ideally, envisioning starts the process of engaging others in executing the plan to make the vision real.

Victor Frankl, the psychologist who survived the Nazi concentration camps and Dr Mengele's experimentation, stated: "Human beings can understand and endure any what if they can answer the question why." His horrific and unique experience taught him that regardless of the situation, you can endure almost anything if you can to some extent understand it. The critical question is *why*. This understanding of human need led him to found the school of logo therapy focusing on the nature of exploring meaning. In all our endeavors we need to have some response when we're challenged: Tell me why?

What does this change mean to the business, why this activity and not another, why me? Great leaders who can re-energize people answer this fundamental question honestly and consistently. Usually, resistance to change is 80% about the why and merely 20% about what and how. So, in the early stages of leading change the focus of attention is clearly on explaining why. This is something which is generally not done well and certainly not done nearly enough. Knowing why isn't the same as explaining why to other people.

If the leader can't explain the context of what they are doing and why they are doing it, then it becomes almost impossible to get others excited and energized about it. If you can't be passionate about your mission, why should someone who works for you be? If you want to build real understanding and commitment, think why, and then, think how.

The leader needs to answer the why question for themselves and their followers. Failure to do so means that they can't face the team, their department or the business with sincerity and answer the questions that invariably will be asked about their direction and vision. A $3^e$ leader is clear on these at least for him- or herself and then finds a way, the story, to share with others.

## Entertaining why

Leading change is tough, but no one said it had to be dull. Collectively sharing a vision of the future is individually stimulating and hugely collaborative. People begin to more clearly understand the aspirations of their colleagues and their leader. The synthesis of these ideas isn't a homogenization, or some crude reduction to common denominators, but a plus, plus, plus – a process that builds up a compelling and truly shared vision. It's this collective process that's the strength of the methodology. Carried out with some energy and invention it's also great fun! Indeed, making strategy meetings entertaining should be at the top of every leader's agenda. Remember what Einstein said: "Creativity is just intelligence having fun."

Envisioning is getting everyone on the starting blocks in the race for change, knowing what the race is about, what the distance is, how many hurdles there are en route. Most importantly, it's about telling everyone what the prize is for winning. Given that most change processes and most organizational strategic plans are marathons, then leaders must learn how to sustain morale and help people run at the most effective pace.

There are three contributing elements to envisioning:

**Competence** – defining the challenges and opportunities that the organization faces and that the team is going to take on to make change happen;

**Context** – framing of these challenges in the organization's corporate religion and current situation;

**Challenges** – defining the goals of the organization, the things that will be delivered to get to the desired future.

Working through these elements both as a leader and in collaboration with others is the process of envisioning.

## Envisioning Sony

We developed some of the framework while coaching senior teams in Sony Europe. Working with one of the leadership teams responsible for the Sony Like No Other™ campaign we helped them explore what a company like no other would really be like. This strap line was conceived by Tokyo's central marketing group as the first truly global marketing campaign. In Europe, Like No Other seemed like a great opportunity to create a call to arms, a way to lift and inspire, engage and encourage the people who worked for the company. Sony wanted to be truly like no other company. This meant engaging with the sometime skeptical employees in a way that would embrace the idea of uniqueness, maverick thinking, being out front and being different.

The executive team of Sony Europe saw this as a chance to create a new future for the business and to refresh the values and spirit of the brand. Management clearly intended like.no.other to be more than a strap-line. It was seen as a genuine opportunity to banish boredom and defy dullness. The new manifesto for how to be "like. us" read:

*We are more than a business and more than a brand.*
*We are an idea, a dream, a philosophy, a spirit,*
*We share a different view of the world,*
*We're not here to be logical or predictable,*
*We do what other's don't,*
*We enjoy new thinking, explore the impossible and pursue the unknown,*
*We're optimistic, playful and ingenious,*
*We wonder, we question, and we create . . .*
*For every no, we see "yes"*
*For every stop, we say "go"*
*For every off, we turn "on"*
*When others ask "why?", we say "why not?"*
*We are like no other*

Our first task was to enable teams to move beyond a stirring vision on a piece of paper. This was a two-part process. First, we stimulated the creation of the big picture dream. We wanted to help them get a real view of the company in the future – a dream that would make practical sense and have a deadline. As noted in Part One, it remains a constant surprise to us how little time is devoted in large organizations to really thinking deeply about the future. We chose to do this as facilitated debate. We provoked brainstorming, discussion and, inevitably, some argument, based on ideas of the current world and future trends. It wasn't a superficial process, but one that really challenged them to think.

As a creative thinker once told us, "You can open the door to change and ask people to walk through, but sometimes it's more effective to pull them in from the other side." In working with Sony we exposed its key people to an inner and outer context – the wider world view and the internal view of the world – the corporate religion and the harsh new realities.

By analyzing the outer context – the impact of changes in technology, institutions and values in society, business as well as in the industries in which Sony is active – we enabled the team to make connections between the points they could spot on the greater socio-economic landscape. So, exploring what the take up of broadband in Europe was doing to the way people interacted, the way they shared media, they way they watched or didn't watch television, was one example of the impact of technology on consumer behavior. Think of joining the dots pictures you might have done as a child. We placed lots of dots on the paper and helped them join the right ones up.

Not having the answers, but having the right questions allowed us to introduce some trends and emerging behaviors that Sony would need to understand if they were to remain like no other but in a positive rather than negative way.

The inner context was then described aided by the seven dimensions of Sony's corporate religion. This structure allowed us to share the teams thinking about the identity of the organization in a way they had never previously considered. Was the corporate religion of Sony really like no other, and if not, what would make it so?

At Sony, one of the most interesting elements was the mythology surrounding the company and some of its individuals. One of Sony's most recent iconic myths concerns Ken Kutaragi, the engineer and inventor of the PlayStation games console. He was not given official clearance to develop the chip and console set that Sony were making for another supplier. He went with his ideas for a 3D gaming console to his superiors and was told bluntly, "Sony don't make toys." For most this would have been final, but for Kutaragi it was just a small set back. Believing in his dream, he "borrowed", cajoled, found and possibly loaned without consent, resources from around Sony to pursue his project. Within Sony the tale of the "non-project" is told regularly, not formally but by colleagues when explaining why Sony is like it is. These non-projects are sometimes referred to as submarines, silently going about their mission but prepared to surface when ready.

PlayStation is now the dominant games platform in the world and the most profitable single product Sony has ever conceived. PlayStation 3, the latest evolution, leads the pack, some 20 years since the submarine left its dock.

Of course, religions have cathedrals, mosques and temples. Sony, like many large corporations, has iconic buildings. Sony's European headquarters in Berlin is visited by more people each year than the Reichstag or the Brandenburg Gate. There are other iconic buildings across the globe fulfilling the same function, a symbol of status and belief in the brand and organization. These icons are as important to the employees as they are to the outside world. External and internal context matters.

Exploring what existed already and what meaning people attached to them, was only a starting point. We then asked the team to let the two contexts interact in their minds. From this synthesis, they were invited to think about what business opportunities and challenges existed for Sony in the light of the changes and the internal strengths of the organization. It was mental scenario planning on steroids.

To encourage the teams to focus more "fixedly", but remain in a flexible and open state, we introduced them to the Lou Reed method (see box). Team members were encouraged to describe a Perfect Day in the Sony of the future. The result was a colorful, compelling, down-to-earth, and shared picture of the future, and one collaboratively created and owned by the whole of the team.

Mostly, our dreams are personal and rarely shared. Using something more creative such as the Lou Reed method, we can create an ambience and a structure where that sharing of emotionally important ideas is safe and also exciting. Taking a glimpse at the possible is always exciting when you're part of the creation of the dream. Of course, the idea of perfection varies from person to person, but if the process is performed well, it creates a vivid view of the world of work in which everyone is firing on all cylinders.

**Bright Idea No. 1 – The Lou Reed Method – creative guided thinking**

To create a future that's better than the one people currently experience then you need to find a way for them to be creative and free from restricted thinking. We created a guided journey into a Perfect Day in the future, where they are at work (wherever that may be) and have a fantastic working day, everything going right, enjoyable but challenging. We know from research that challenge and enjoyment are the psychological requirements that create the mental state of FLOW. When people are in flow they perform to their personal best.

The individuals take turns to share these images with their fellow team mates, verbally giving a rich description of what they are doing, who with, what the customers are saying and how their day is taken up. This is something that can seem risky at times and very emotionally involved. However, if you set up the place and the timing right, it can be a very powerful method. We use the track "Perfect Day" in the background, and use some carefully selected, well placed, encouraging questions to aid calm reflection. Done in a comfortable place, with some respect but also a sense of fun and exploration it's a great way to access people's depth of imagination. This is an exercise for opening minds and hearts at the same time. You can see the physiological change in people as they place themselves in that ideal work place doing that which they are excellent at. It's this future state that's important not only to invoke but also capture.

As Disney said: "All our dreams can come true, if we have the courage to pursue them."

When using this approach with a work team there's surprising overlap and also surprising differences. What you help the team create is a shared view (the overlaps) of what perfect working conditions mean for their company and their team, and to think about the diversity and options to explore and develop (the differences). A debate and dialogue naturally flows about what the future should be and what that would mean for the people in the organization. Just a perfect day.

## Blurred vision

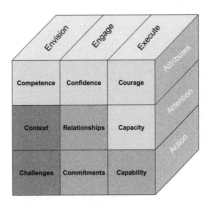

*Steve was chief engineer at a large manufacturing site of a global fast moving consumer goods (FMCG) company. He was a high energy manager getting a lot of things moving all at once. His initial impact with his bosses and peers was very positive. A bright guy, with a first class degree, Steve was full of ideas and strategies, but he was difficult to influence because of his quick thinking. If you couldn't keep up, he regarded it as your problem. Steve did not really see the need to include others in his envisioning process. Given his approach, he had a tendency to burn out people around him. They couldn't always keep up with his thinking and found it difficult to challenge him on issues where they had counter views.*

*Steve lived in a world with little dissent. One by one his team members gave up trying to influence him. They were unwilling to undergo the pressure of attempting to change his mind. They swung from being completely engaged and excited by this whirlwind leader, to being under pressure, mis-aligned and cynical, not because they did not want to do a good job but because they no longer understood why they were doing what they were doing. They had lost their connection to the context of the organization/function. They didn't have any ownership of the challenges that the engineering department were facing.*

*Steve was moved to another smaller part of the organization, after stalling three years into his position in the chief engineer's role. He seemed unable to keep people with him over time. Unable to share his vision and the context behind it, people lost trust and faith in him. An individual with clear passion and at times brilliant ideas to improve his part of the business crashed and burned because of his failure to build a shared vision with his team.*

# 16   Elements of envisioning

## The importance of intelligence

When we built the model we were sure that there are three core attributes of leaders: Competence, Confidence and Courage. We will deal with each of these in detail in the relevant chapters. However, it's useful to have a set of test questions in your mind as you consider these:

- Is the person smart enough to understand the business, at both the strategic and operational level?
- Do they have the ability and confidence to build strong relationships with people at all levels?
- Are they driven to make things happen for themselves and for the business?

As noted earlier, envisioning is the process of creating that shared picture of the future with your team and other significant players around you. Leading this process means using your competence – the intellectual horsepower you possess – to define the critical strategic issues facing the organization. It's a mix of rational analysis and creative exploration focused on the future.

In order to do this well, we believe re-energizing leaders need to be smart in three ways – able to see patterns and trends in data across a wide landscape, dig deep into relevant details of the business and finally be open to the possibility of learning. Sum these attributes up and you have competence.

Competence, as we define it, is fluid and generative, while knowledge is more historic, experience-based and relatively static. Re-energizing leaders need to use their competence to generate with others, in a way that they truly get it, compelling visions of tomorrow. Intellectual curiosity is essential.

We've by default suggested that $3^e$ leaders need to have reasonable levels of intellectual ability. We're not talking about IQ off the scales. Indeed, we're not really thinking about the standard definition of IQ. We're not suggesting that levels of genius are necessary, but that it's about leaders being smart. (You'll see in the later chapter on developing leaders what we suggest in terms of selection mechanisms and how to develop leadership in your population.)

A few attributes contribute significantly to leadership success in re-energizing in practice and these attributes can be identified generically. Most competency frameworks already have them buried in the morass of paperwork and online selection tools. We believe there are only a critical few and that they disproportionately and positively affect the results leaders get.

## Smarter than the average bear

The key attribute leaders bring to the envisioning process is intellectual competence; a creative mix of strategic thinking and analytical ability. It's raw IQ to some extent, learning what needs to be learnt, rather than just static knowledge. In most organizations, leaders are accountable for defining success. This was certainly true in our experience of working with many large international and some smaller domestic organizations.

It's not a given that people with an IQ score of 130 will always be successful in business. In fact some are too smart to want to work for someone else. However, the probability of people with a relatively low IQ, or even an average one, being able to lead a business and lead the new demanding breed of organizational man isn't high.

It's a hard truth for some people to hear but smart people make better leaders in 99% of the cases. We see from recent years of elections that some western voters seem to want to test this theory, but given a choice opt for candidates to run your business that have a good IQ score, and by this we mean in the top quartile of the population, not just those hovering above the average. It sounds harsh and not very politically correct, but face facts, if intelligence isn't really important why do we test for it in university entry, school selection exams, the army and the government service? We're not talking about qualifications. Churchill, Einstein and other great leaders from the past have proved the value of original thinking over and above the evidence of exams. In our view, mental horsepower adds the essential spark to leaders.

Nine questions to ask about your **Competence**:

- Do I understand more about my industry than most of my peers?
- Do I regularly read management and business books to find new ideas?
- Can I make good decisions with limited or ambiguous data?
- Do I enjoy working on future scenarios for my business even if they are hypothetical?
- Do I enjoy working on complex problems that require new solutions?
- Can I quickly see the crucial issue in any situation?
- Can I see patterns in complex data more easily than my peers?
- Do I understand what needs to be done to make the business better?
- Do I have a clear long-term plan for the business I have responsibility for?

## Beyond bored rooms

Compelling pictures of the future rarely come from boardroom décor. To ignite energy, it's vital that the work environment feeds into the other elements of the vision. Remember, an organization that proclaims to be unique, innovative and different, with people miraculously producing creative work can only be achieved, if the physical dimension is also catered for. We believe that it's important to create an environment to stimulate, excite and entertain the impossible.

Consider both real spaces *and* psychological spaces. We all understand the requirement for real estate space for a business to operate, but what's psychological space all about? It's not so different in some respects. It boils down to having space to think the unthinkable, and confidence in the ability to explore what's not the norm. In many organizations that become successful, management tries to codify the means of success – growing large policy documents, process charts and other means to reduce the space to think and act independently. Think McDonalds – same taste guaranteed – high on predictability, but low on surprise.

Re-energized organizations need some mental space – freedom from the ministry of truth – to challenge and contest. If this space doesn't exist in the minds of the people you're trying to work with then we suggest you start to make it. If you have people saying frequently in your meetings, "but that just won't work in this organization," "that's not going to get approved" or even "they would never allow that" then you know there's not enough psychological space to really embrace change. We're sure many of you have run computers at times crammed so full of defunct programs, deleted files and the general detritus of day-to-day work that they run like sloths on valium. Freeing up this memory revives performance and speed. Think about it, if your people are running with burdens and restrictions of the defunct past, maybe it is time to reboot.

Re-energizing the way people think is first about opening up their minds to possibilities that they have never considered. Following this principle has required us to do some strange things to the décor of conference rooms we worked in and even stranger things to the team's collective view of the world of work. If you want to change people positively then you have to model the process yourself first. In our experience running workshops about challenging the future dressed like a grey suited auditor, power pointing the audience into submission isn't the way to lead a real dialogue about the possible. Make your stimulus material omnipresent. Flooding the working space (our abused conference rooms) with all and everything connected to the issues you're dealing with means that people can access the images, data and thinking at any time, not some slot prescribed by consultants. This is a way of really embracing the freedom of information legislation. Giving people choices to get involved rather than consequences for not, is far more empowering and effective. We also think that modeling yourself the new ways of working as well as describing them is far more effective in getting real change.

Examining the wider context of change starts to frame the possibilities you explore with reference to the current situation, the competition, the environment, the community, the industry and critically other people in the room. We've experienced change programs that either don't understand the need for context or don't value time spent on it, and they are extremely difficult processes to sustain. The human animal needs to know why and how. Both are rooted in knowing the context.

Re-energizing leaders have to embrace this idea of exploration and explanation. Generation Choice needs data to make their decisions. Sharing the context of change provides the data that will enable them to make their decision one to follow and not one to flee. We know that given the right data in the right way most smart people make the right decisions.

Nine questions to ask about your ability to set the **Context**:

- Do I believe all employee targets should be linked directly to strategic issues?
- Do my team members understand how we contribute to the wider business plan?
- Do I meet regularly to talk with team members about the direction of the business?

- Can my team members have direct involvement in creating strategic direction for my area?
- Do my team members know what the most important business issues are over the next three years?
- Do my team members see how meeting these goals and objectives meet customer needs?
- Can I explain these issues clearly to my team?
- Is everyone in my team clear about why we pursue this particular strategy?
- Do my team members understand that their success is dependent on other parts of the business as much as internal activity?

## The leadership challenge

It's execution we're all paid for and results that we're remembered by. But those results start with clear ideas of what the challenge is. Remember the importance of goal clarity from positive psychology. You'd be surprised how many managers we meet who can't articulate why they are in their role, their purpose in the business. If you don't believe us ask some of your colleagues – and be prepared to be surprised.

The challenges the leaders select may initially be set at a high level and ultimately require more detail, but they set the agenda for the team, department or corporation. The leader's role is to translate strategy and the overall corporate dream into something much more operational and concrete; into terms that teams and individuals can understand, get involved in and execute. Challenges are the "what's to be done" element of the leader's tenure. These can be very specific in terms of targets and deadlines, as in some major project, or they can be more conceptual in terms of creative roles. Regardless of the nature, specific or conceptual, they should be ambitious. No one is energized by mediocrity or trying slightly harder. Energizing others takes a clear challenge, not a polite request.

That's why we call them challenges and not just goals. They should be seen as a set of actions or targets that others in your team and others concerned within your organization can clearly identify with. By ambitious we mean a stretch in scale or scope in comparison with the current or past. So, getting to number one in the market you serve is ambitious if you're habitually fifth, but just reactive if you were number one last year.

For one organization that we're currently helping re-energize the challenge is to increase four fold within four years the placement of disadvantaged and disabled job seekers into sustainable mainstream employment. This particular government institution needs to achieve this against a background of capped funding and an increasingly more demanding client base. This particular organizational challenge has both scope and stretch. What they know already is that to meet this challenge they will have to re-energize their leadership, their people and their way of thinking about employment practices. Staying as they are isn't an option and will only result in slow and painful demise. The price if they don't succeed is the resulting loss of a service that unlocks a truly enormous hidden potential in society and makes a difference to thousands of individuals.

We call these the leadership challenges, but in effect they are the change challenges of the organization not just of the leadership. Challenges are the strategic goals that people and organizations understand. Defining these change challenges and crafting from them the right strategic goals are core leadership actions. Later in the book we'll share some creative and pragmatic ways of doing this. The quality of your leadership starts with the quality of your goal setting and the ambition of the challenges you set. Are your challenges both clear and ambitious? Are you ambitious enough? Stretch!

Nine questions to ask about the way you define **Challenges**:

- Do the goals and objectives for my team address both short-term and long-term business needs?
- Do my team members understand the impact of the goals and objectives for the business?
- Have I broken down the overall challenges into operational goals?
- Will delivery on these goals and objectives have strategic impact on the business?
- Does every team member have a clear view of the way the challenge makes a difference to the business?
- Are consequences of failure and benefits of success clear to all?
- Do my team members believe that the challenges we face are achievable but ambitious?
- Can I describe how to overcome the challenges set for myself and my team members?
- Are my personal goals and challenges linked to the development of the business and not just operational issues?

## Back to the future – Part II

It's by building on the ideologies of the existing corporate religion that re-energizing leaders help shape the dreams of what could and should be. A great starting point in creating compelling pictures of the future is to build on the plusses that are already there. People are much more inclined to believe in something that they can see and hear is connected to what they already know and are comfortable with. If you want to influence others to move forward with you, you have to move them from common ground. The existing corporate religion, the culture they already understand is that common base and the best starting point.

We see organizational rituals and totems all around us that symbolize who we are and what we stand for. It would be a very brave leader who would tear them down and then ask his people to support change. Leading others requires that they connect with you and see you as a leader, not as a heretic.

We know from research on how people react to change that the majority of us like to see a causal path, from where we are now, to where we want to be. The link to the future must be one that the critical mass'of people in the organization can grasp, at the conceptual level, before they act at the operational level. People require more than a rallying cry and a shout of "Let's just do it" from their leaders. Leading change requires you as a leader to touch not only the intellectual needs people have for understanding, their minds, but also their emotional needs, their hearts.

All change starts with the individual, and then with the team and then the organization. In our experience, the most important individual, at the envisioning stage at least, is the leader of the senior group. Sometimes this is the president or CEO, but more often change is driven at a divisional or country level. It's important for leaders and their teams, whatever the level of the organization, to go through some form of envisioning process. Without this, the probability of organizational change being successful is extremely small.

**Individual Change - Focus on the challenge to be overcome**

*and then*

**Team Change – Focus on a shared picture of the challenge**

*and then*

**Organizational Change – Start implementing concrete plans**

Envisioning requires you to move from the level of working with the individual to embracing the whole organization. In an attempt to help organizations develop leadership among their senior people, we focus on working with a small number of management teams who have significant challenges or major strategic influence. A sense of urgency matters. If you get enough of these teams to work in a new aligned direction, then the organizational super tanker starts to alter course, slowly but surprisingly. The good example matter. Experiment!

## 17    Engage

## Opening doors in your mind

A colleague told us a story about a newly appointed CEO. When he arrived in the old fashioned building he was to be based in, he was shocked to find a series of corridors and small private offices. He knew he'd taken on the role to revitalize the company but didn't expect it to be stuck in the dark ages. He came from a place with spacious, light, open plan offices which enhanced communication and gave a buzz to the company. He also knew that spending money on HQ refurbishment would send out the wrong message to the struggling company's many hard working employees.

In his frequent early meetings he encouraged his new team and their managers to adopt an open door policy to show that regardless of the design of the building, they were always on hand to talk to. He would often walk into the office coming back from meeting a customer to find doors closed while their occupants held meetings, made phone calls or just wanted to shut out interruptions. He made a point of opening every one he saw closed, to be met with embarrassed and flustered managers apologizing for forgetting to keep the door open.

One month in, the CEO took unilateral action. He came in during the weekend with a small team of builders who took every office door off its hinges and stacked them in the car park in skips. The fire doors were the only survivors.

Monday came with the shock to his team that he had planned and expected. They passed familiar doors stacked in builder's skips. While on their way into the building the CEO just mentioned to those brave enough to ask that as they seemed to forget to leave their doors open as they all agreed, he thought he would help them by removing the problem.

Later that day his private secretary came to see him. An old hand of the company and a loyal supporter of her boss, but a confidant of many in the senior ranks, she asked if she could have a quiet word.

"I fully agree with what you've done, and it's absolutely the right thing to do for everyone. Everyone that is, except you. I sit right outside your office, next to where the door used to be, and you have lots of important guests and make very important and sensitive phone calls, which I can overhear. I really think you should have your door re-fitted", she said "It's just not right."

The CEO smiled and with a gentle tone to his voice said, "Thank you for telling me, but if you can hear enough to know it's sensitive, then you know enough not to listen. The doors stay off."

Opening the door to engagement is critical to re-energizing. Engagement isn't just about getting people on board. It's about helping them take part and make contributions meaningful to them and the business. This defines the difference between leadership and management most clearly: managers control, while leaders gain followers who then engage others to take part in building the future of the business. After the You-volution, it's power with, rather than power over.

Once again there are three elements in the Engagement process;

**Confidence** – the mix of self-belief that sends out a message of re-assurance to others, and the trust that confident leaders place in others and that these people place in the leader;

**Relationships** – the network of close and more remote individual connections that allow the leader to have influence;

**Commitments** – the specific contracts (implicit and explicit) that the leader makes with people to enlist their energies in the delivery of change.

## Harry – understated talent

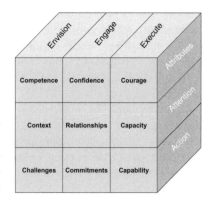

*Harry was a board member of a European technology organization, having joined the business with a background in information technology and systems commissioning. He was not a typically out going person and Harry found it difficult to bang the corporate drum and rally the troops when leading teams. It was*

*just not his style. Simply, his considerable reputation was built on getting things done.*

*The complex international matrix that Harry operated in meant that there were multiple stakeholders and lots of history to every change project that the organization started. Many change efforts taken on by the leadership team failed to materialize as baggage in the organization and strong country loyalties stifled progress. What was evident was Harry's success. In stark contrast to many of his peers, he was able to deliver, time and time again. Recognizing the strength in his ability to organize, for people management and strategic thinking, the president made Harry the owner of the biggest and most complex restructuring, re-engineering and re-organizing effort that the European business had ever attempted in its extensive history.*

*Harry was not fazed at all, but did what he always did on large change projects. He assembled a team of experts he trusted, got clear sign off about the plan from every stakeholder no matter what the investment in time and travel needed to get it, and measured success and learning every day.*

*Harry's experience had taught him that getting the right people mattered and he spent time finding them in the organization and personally talking to them about the need to work on this mammoth project. He had a knack of getting the right hot buttons for each person. So, he would tell some people that they were the only ones skilled enough to do the role. With others it was that they were the only ones with the guts to take the challenge on. He was the master of individualization when talking to his team.*

*Finding the right mix was chapter one in his book. Getting them to build a plan with him was always chapter two. He used his contacts to find a facilitator who could channel the energy of the team in a high-commitment, high-challenge team building and project planning process that created a bit of friction. Harry knew that managing talented people caused a bit of friction, but all work created friction, it's a law of physics.*

*In this business Harry had a reputation for hard work, great planning and delivery. He also had a reputation for building talent and careers. Working with Harry got you noticed and most often, being part of successful delivery, promoted. He had no trouble getting a team to work for him.*

*Knowing the change project was a long haul commitment, as most significant re-engineering projects are, he ensured he had the right measures and feedback mechanisms. Harry set aside every Friday morning for a series of net meetings. He knew that managing a pan-European team with outsourced partners in India would be hard on travel, so he used cyber meetings to measure, coach, report and update everyone. He spent four hours every Friday being available online to each of the 20 or so sub team projects.*

*The team worked hard to impress Harry and not let their other team members down. They understood the importance of what they were doing and how this would have an effect on the profitability of the business and the customer experience. They also knew that if they delivered, there was some reward and increased status for them. When credits and plaudits were called for, Harry ensured those that did the work gained the recognition for it, not him.*

*The re-engineering program was planned for three years, but was delivered in just over 25 months. The savings to the organization therefore increased above forecasts to over 250 million euros. Harry had once again proved that he was capable of leading change in a complex organization, regardless of the internal politics and history of failures. He was a master of engagement and delivery.*

*There's an epilogue. The organization failed to retain Harry's interest and, eventually, lost him. Harry thrived on big challenges and when he had delivered on most of them, found the company less satisfying. In an attempt to keep him, the organization gave him a flexible deal allowing him a 60% contract with 40% time to run his own business start up. This worked for a year but Harry needed his next big challenge and left to go to a smaller technology company, for a much reduced salary. Why? It operated in the green sector, providing technology solutions that were ecologically sound, safe and simple. The challenge turned him on.*

# Elements of
# 18 engagement

## Follow me

The starting point of engagement is confidence, the ability to engender followership from others. This isn't just a phenomenon within the leader's team but a way in which re-energizing leaders influence people in all their relationships. It's a fact that most of us tend to warm to confident people who are able to express themselves clearly and appear to have some conviction. You can respect someone who's confident about themselves and their ideas even if these are opposed to yours. It's this attribute that we believe is important and possibly the most critical element to getting things done in organizations. If you do not have the relationship skills to influence others then organizational life can be very hard indeed.

A second facet of confidence is self-efficacy, or self belief. If as a leader you constantly doubt your own ability this is evident to others and comes out in all the non-verbal signals that you emit during your interactions. It's not something that's controllable or even conscious, just a fact of the way humans communicate.

Professor Albert Mehrabian of UCLA did a study in the 1970s that showed that 38% of the influence you had was by the tone and pitch of your voice, 55% from the body language shown and only 7% was from the words used. Self belief leaks from us, to our audience, either in floods when we have it, or in droplets when we don't. Given a choice people believe what the body language tells them, not the words used. What's more important to recognize is that most of the recognition of body language is done at a sub-conscious level of processing, so we're not aware of why we trust and follow some people, but we have a strong gut feeling that they are credible. That's why some people seem to have charisma and respect and others do not.

You don't need to hear what leaders say to know whether they are credible. Our faces and our bodies give away more than our words ever can. Think again of Bush in that school room upon hearing of the news of 9/11. What did you believe was going on?

Confidence can be regarded as the emotional aspect of leadership. Emotional intelligence has emerged as the phrase used to capture the softer people skills that successful people seem to apply with real impact. It's the mix of relationship building skills, high level communication and empathy that some people seem to have naturally and some have to work hard to develop. In our experience, the process requires a genuine curiosity about what drives and motivates others. If you have no real interest in people then it's going to be incredibly difficult to fake it consistently enough to take others on a change journey.

Many organizations select their leaders mainly on intellectual capacity and results. These are easier to measure than the "softer" attributes of a leadership. Given the enormous importance of psychological performance boosters, we think this completely underestimates the nature of leadership and better efforts should be made to measure the impact of the softer elements of a leader's behavior on others.

Some of the studies on Emotional Intelligence suggest that it's *the* differentiating factor in the success of very high performers in a variety of roles. EQ is important, but we also believe that there needs to be a framework to apply this emotional savvy. The $3^e$ model allows you to focus your positive psychological capabilities in an effective way – on engaging others and executing change.

Success as a leader boils down to the interactions you have with teams, sponsors and peers. Leaders must develop clear, open, honest and strong relationships marked by trust and mutual respect. If the leader displays confidence in what people are doing and shares the context of why they are doing it, the environment necessary for trust to develop is in place. Being confident also allows you to hire and use talented people around you, without fear of being overtaken.

As we've noted, increasingly, companies realize that they need to hire leaders for will just as much as for skill. Much of this will is displayed by confidence in their ability and the belief that they display in their teams. Engagement is really about people choosing to follow you as a leader, making a positive decision to commit to you, not begrudgingly comply because of some financial or punitive consequence.

A re-energizing leader uses confidence and individually adapted stories to attract commitment from each and every person. They know that just appealing to the masses with some one-size-fits-all process won't do. We're not suggesting that the CEO of Mega Inc. goes around talking to each and every one of the 200000+ staff, but we're definitely recommending that the direct reports, key stakeholders and significant others do get a lot of face time and attention. You can't influence all the people in your organization in a meaningful way from the top, but as a leader you can do it by proxy if you get your message tailored for your own team.

In developing their skills of engagement, we often urge leaders to define an EVP – an employee value proposition – a summary of the experience the organization is trying to impart to people. Usually, the EVP simply evolves. It emerges as an aggregation of all that happens to an employee. It's been created over time and, most often, unconsciously. Not many companies take the time to think about the work experience they are building for their staff. Those that do this consciously find it a revealing and worthwhile exercise and one that invariably leads to them examining their EVP for the future. Remember, real talent has the choice to walk and will do so if they aren't doing something that's valued and worthwhile. Money and status are no longer the shackles they used to be.

Building the relationship with the critical people in your network is essential to having the influence to lead. It's also important to somehow engage the others in the organization particularly if the change you're leading is affecting their daily behavior.

Nine questions to ask about your **Confidence**:

- Am I regularly asked to speak at meetings to give a view on matters not within my responsibility?
- Am I trusted with confidential information by my peers and my boss?
- Do I enjoy influencing groups by presenting or talking to them at meetings?
- Does my team confide in me about work related problems without being asked?
- Do I have a strong relationship with the senior team and am able to challenge their thinking?
- Can I openly acknowledge when I do not have the answer?
- Can I challenge people's ideas when I do not understand, regardless of their seniority?
- Am I happy to admit when I am wrong, even in a group situation?
- Am I sure when I have made a good decision about people?

## Friends and relations

The fact that everyone is unique and has different needs and motives means that the engagement process is built up of a collection of individual relationships. We know about the problem with being able to choose your friends but not your relations, but in the organizational world you can and should chose both. The relationships you build will determine the results that you achieve. Choose carefully.

The way you relate to others is important and should be in line with your core values. What we mean is that it should be sincere. The way you interact with those influential in the delivery of change will determine how successful you are. The way you demonstrate your confidence and determination will either inspire others to embrace your plans or conspire to make them fail. It really is that critical. Your leadership is a personal thing to each and every person you have a working relationship with. They may all see you in different ways, giving and taking different things from them. What a good leader realizes is that all the people they work with are unique and require a individualized approach to getting the best from them.

Researchers at Rutgers University in the United States have shown that contrary to expectation and intuition the more you customize your response to individuals in terms of contract, development, reward and incentives, the more productive the organization becomes. The days of economies of scale in performance management, contracts, bonus schemes, benefits and pay are in their opinion numbered. There's a huge caveat: you need to ensure that you individualize the work contract, for the right people. In their experience this is clearly the "A" players in your organization, who you then deploy into "A" roles.

Their work suggests that careful selection of talent, as opposed to the scatter gun approach, is critical to business success. Not only does this mean finding and grading talent, it means that you must individualize the deal with them as well. This is the age of the new psychological contract – answering "what's in it for me" has never been more important if you're to retain the talent your business needs.

Some of the most important relationships are with the individuals within your team and the people who you report to. These may be non-executives or the chairman at one end of the scale or your functional head at the other. However, your ability to manage successful relationships with these people directly affects your success at delivery. In terms of the individual leaders' career and reputation, delivery is what matters. The corporate Hall of Fame is filled with people who have excelled at executing. Rarely do you make the corporate history books if you fail, unless you fail big time.

So **how** do you build strong and honest relationships with the people you need to?

The skill associated with relationship building is the ability to personalize your approaches and build trust. A $3^e$ leader thinks about and listens for the signs of what drives others and gives them a sense of purpose that fits their values. With this knowledge they can then ensure that they relate to the individual in a way that makes sense to them and connects to their needs.

In terms of making connections with others, leaders capable of re-energizing take the other person as the starting point, and think about why the other person should be interested in their goals, in their projects. Using this as a staring point, rather than themselves, seems to ensure that they can really relate and understand others who may or may not be useful in their careers.

A friend of ours told us of a time when her father had the great fortune to be seated next to Nelson Mandela at a gala dinner connected with his professional role in football. She told us of her father saying that even though they had never met before he felt that when talking to the great man he was given his undivided attention as though he was the most important thing to him.

The networking leader is someone who can call on favors, find resources, learn where the decisions are being made and get intelligence on what the competition is doing. Being well connected is a way of working. It's not something that's manipulative, just highly influential. The wider your net, the more fish you can catch.

Having the ability to network and build relationships isn't something that's soft or fluffy but something that experience shows is a critical factor in successful leadership. One of the managers we coach said, "but I'm not one for small talk and just having lunch with people, its not me." We're not advocating that you try to become the equivalent of the local priest or shopping mall greeter. Instead, work out who you need in your network and find practical ways in which to bring them in, close and connected to you.

## Wondrous stories

Story telling is one way of connecting messages to people outside of your immediate network. We see and encourage stories as an important tool of the engagement process. Stories provide the link between change, continuity and causality. They also provide a means to engage people in the culture, myths and myths yet to written about the organization.

When people talk about submarine projects in Sony, everyone knows exactly what they are talking about – and it's not submarines! More importantly, those same people relate to how in the past major products have come from these non projects cruising below the surface of the real organization. Stories make points with impact and often humor that policy and procedure will never match. They simply carry more sway than spin.

Engagement is an emotional process, and stories convey emotion better than factual pieces. Part of the engagement process therefore concerns building the new storybook of the organization. When we worked on the like.no.other project, at Sony the stories told were still too much about the past glories and not enough about the current successes. Now, a new communication style is very much part of a re-energized Sony, with a special channel devoted to the task. @SONY is a netcast tool to spread the word within the Sony world and show who's and how to be like.no.other.

Nine questions to ask about your **Relationships**:

- Do I have a good network of peers and colleagues inside the company?
- Do I seek feedback from both internal and external customers about our performance and what could be done to make it better?
- Do I have a good open working relationship with my boss?
- Do my team members trust my judgment on work issues?
- Am I seen by my peers as an excellent communicator?
- Do I spend a lot of my time talking to people about their work and listen to their ideas?
- Do I enjoy coaching others to better performance and take time to do it?
- Do I regularly seek opinions and views from others before taking important decisions?
- Do I care how my peers perceive me?

## The rituals of engagement

Along with stories comes the use of rituals. We've observed that $3^e$ leaders make extensive use of rituals to engage their followers. In a European research center, R&D team members lamented the fact that no one had organized the company barbeque. When we explored this seemingly small issue it became clear what incredible status this event held in the minds of these brilliant and highly regarded researchers. It was their one time to share with their families what they did at work and meet colleagues in a truly informal and non-hierarchical manner. The center had not organized the event because of work pressures. There was nothing intentional, it just never got done. When the team met to discuss the long term strategy for the business and how to motivate the staff the whole issue came out.

The event ran this year and is now recognized as a core and cost effective tool in the motivation and team building of this center.

Engagement is built on the lasting relationships that the leader builds in the organization. Knowing who to know and who should be in our network are critical questions for leaders. In many large organizations, people depend on internal networks to get things done as much as formal structures. We've seen really important projects or programs fail because not enough thought or effort has been given to understanding the network and stakeholders involved.

If you ask yourself these questions about your network, do the answers satisfy you and make you confident about your connections?

- Does my team trust me and confide in me when they are concerned?
- Do my peers seek out my opinions and advice?
- Is there anyone who can stall my progress I have no relationship with?
- Are there people who unnecessarily demand too much of my time?

Working with change leaders we recommend that they map out their networks and identify the people that they have in their influence, and those that they don't but should. This exercise, drawn out initially on blank flip charts is sometimes a startling revelation.

---

### Bright Idea No. 2 – Circles of Influence

If you don't know who you know, how can you manage relation-ships to ensure you're successful in leading change? We all have circles of influence – some formal given by position and rank, and many more informal given by history, shared interests, debts, favors and recommendations. If you want to really make an impact in change leadership you should know who to bring into your camp, who may not be there, and how to influence the ones who already are there.

Take a large blank canvas; a flip chart pad is ideal, but the back of a poster or a large format paper will do. A3 is probably the smallest which will work well.

Draw a circle in the center with your name or initials in the middle. Then, start to map the surrounding space with the names, or if you only know the position/title of the people who are in your network currently. Follow these guiding rules:

–   The most frequent meetings/ interactions should be closer to your circle.
–   The importance of the relationship is shown by size of circle
–   The influence you have is shown by the size of the arrow going from you to them
–   The influence they have over you is shown by the arrow going from them to you.

After some thought, you'll finally have a diagram like the one below representing the current state of your network.

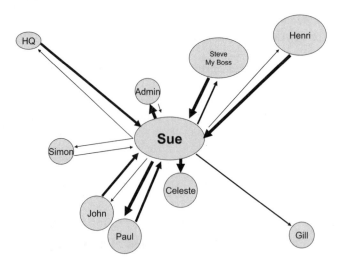

The next step that we encourage people we work with to take is to then think about the distance. Should any be nearer, denoting more frequent interaction? Should any be further away? Should there be anyone on this map who currently isn't there? Are the arrows showing the relationships and influence that you need to be successful? Who should you be more influential with in this network? It's also useful to ask if there are people in the network that shouldn't be there for this project, but demand attention regardless.

We then ask them to update or redraw the map – showing the network that they should have as a change leader.

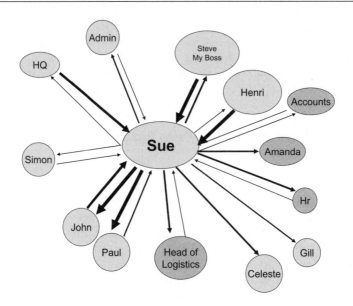

The second map shows the change in line strength denoting reducing or increasing influence, and also some new contacts to make, HR, the Head of Logistics, Accounts and Amanda. The frequency of interactions between Sue and some of the contacts in the network have also changed in this example, as the importance of their relationships changes in the light of leading change.

The next step is deciding what action to take in each case. To move from diagram one to diagram two.

## The wisdom of crowds

The next step after thinking about your personal network concerns how to engage the majority of the people who work in your department or in the organization. It's hard to work on major implementation without the support and involvement of the majority. History has shown us that most attempts to get ideas from the employees are initially treated with suspicion. So, how do you engage people in a way that's sincere, useful and gains their respect?

There are many ways of creating involvement but we've found real benefits from letting go of the normal controls of workshops and letting people work on things that interest them. Open Space Technology (see box below) is one approach to group involvement that really works. It has been used successfully with groups of 15 and with 2000 people. The boundaries are just your level of confidence and some basic preparation. What's essential using this method is that the leader genuinely has the confidence to let others get really involved and doesn't get tempted to wrestle back control mid process. This can have a completely negative impact not only for the event but also for the future trust the team has in the leader. When you give over power to the team, trust them to use it wisely. In our experience, most do.

---

### Bright Idea No. 3 – Open Space Technology

If you really want to engage others, particularly if your organization has a poor record of doing so in the past, then you need to find a way to show your real interest in the opinion of the people who work with you. One method we've used is called Open Space Technology (OST). This is a way of getting some real commitment, involvement and participation of employees on business critical issues. If you want engaged employees then you have to be confident enough to let them take a real part in the business.

OST is essentially a structure for a large problem solving meeting, but one that encourages ownership. It's facilitated but only in a very light way. The simplicity of the method sometimes hides the complexity of the ideas behind them. An OST event is typically one day, where the whole system gets into a room to try to solve some of the systems root problems or challenges. It's a volunteer thing. Only those who want to turn up. The venue is big enough to have all the participants sitting in the same room in a circle of chairs. This isn't a séance but the starting point for shared communication. The main issue is then shared, which takes the form of a question, e.g. "How can we make the customer more satisfied with our deliveries?"

Next is the "market place", essentially a place for placing issues, sub issues and problems that the questions bring up. Individuals post their issues, problems and questions. This wall of "post it notes" becomes the market for issues to solve or discuss. Many are small, some huge and most require some real debate to share, explore and solve. That's the main purpose of OST – to get the people dealing with the issues to find workable solutions to them. Groups form and break up as each issue is dealt with to the level of some agreed conclusion or possible course of action.

As a concept that's about it. There are some things the facilitator does to ensure participation and recording and some basic rules of engagement, but in our experience the show runs on the energy generated by engaged minds.

## The commitments

Engagement is made up of three elements – Confidence, Relationships and Commitments. If you've taken the time as a leader to build the confidence of your immediate team and critical stakeholders and mapped your networks, to know who to influence, then you're in a great position to make things happen. At this stage you'll have the challenges outlined, the context of these challenges clear in your own mind and those of your team, the crucial network of influencers mapped out and connected to your project through your relationships. It's like the stage is all set for action, scene set, players in place, lines learnt and ready for the curtain to be raised. What's missing are the stage directions, the specific instructions and expectations from the director. This is really what the commitment process is all about.

As you'll discover in the process of exploring $3^e$ leadership, explicit commitments are replacing the psychological contracts of old. Open and honest deals are the new glue that binds followers to leaders and leaders to deliver business results. How often in your own career have you tried your hardest to be successful but not really been clear about what's expected of you? There are occasions when working hard is just not enough. If the boss was expecting something different to what you understood they wanted, it's not only frustrating, but it's wasteful of talent and time.

When we talk to leaders and managers about commitments they often say that they understand exactly and "Yes, all my team members know what they are doing and what we're trying to achieve." It's not that we don't believe them, it's just that we're naturally curious about the other perspective, that of the team members.

So we ask the team members the following specific questions:

- What's expected from you on this project?
- Why specifically are you asked to take responsibility for this?
- What will you personally get from it if you're successful?
- What support can you expect to get from your boss to help you?
- What are the consequences of failing to deliver your part of this project?

What we find is that when the leader says people know what they are doing and what's expected of them, it's not as clear as we know it should be. It is worth taking some time to check out the reality.

Let's explain the nature of the questions one by one and see how when taken as a whole they create the conditions for real commitments.

## What is expected from you on this project?

Individuals need to know, and be able to articulate, the task or targets that they think they are working toward. This question gets straight to the heart of that. If there's a gap between what they think, and what you asked of them, then we've uncovered the first reason why you might be disappointed with the process of execution that we've yet to discuss. It's by no means rocket science or brain surgery, but good leadership means understanding that what you've asked for may not always be received by everyone in the same way. Check out that people understand what you asked for. Do not assume they understand what you think you asked for. Clear?

## Why specifically are you asked to take responsibility for this?

This question is about motivation and valuing people in your team for specific contributions. If the answer to the question is "John asked me to do this because he knows that researching options and technical problem solving is what I'm good at and enjoy" then you have won a prize. The key to motivation and peak performance is to put people on what they are good at and enjoy as much as possible. Too often the answer to the question is something like this, "I'm not sure, I presume that John thought there's no one else left with spare time, I guess someone has to do it." You can hear the difference?

Again you don't have to be Abraham Maslow to see that there's potentially a different level of commitment and a different understanding of the leaders' motives. You get high commitment when people are told why they are asked to take something on and why it's important to you and the success of the project. Make it explicit and double-check that they get it!

## What will you personally get from it if you're successful?

We all have a little radio receiver built into our psyche receiving on channel WII fm. This is the station that searches for the signal for What's In It For Me, *WIIFM*. If you want to get people tuned in then transmit on this frequency. We all want an individual play list – some like to know that success on this will give them the visibility in the company that they crave, others the access to the training that they want, with others still it's about career opportunities, bonuses or challenging new experiences. Debate, discuss and do a deal with each individual. What can you do to reward the efforts that you want from them? The more effort you expect the more reward they expect is generally the norm. We know from research, well documented motivation and reward studies, that the reward must meet two criteria; what matters is the value the person receiving it places on it and the probability of them being able to do it. This second point leads us to the next question very neatly.

## What support can you expect to get from your boss to help you?

If we're asked to give some of our discretionary effort, the bit that's freely given when we're engaged, then it must be seen by each of us to be worth it. Even when the reward offered is something that's desirable to us we always mentally check if the conditions, the probability, are favorable to us.

A great prize in a competition that you can't win isn't an incentive. So, the role of the leader in providing genuine support is critical to releasing that discretionary effort. The deal is agreeing "if you do this, to this agreed standard, you'll get x (where x has some value for them as an individual) and the support you can expect from me is y (where y is the support they have asked for in order to feel confident they can achieve)." We do deals all the time in business. Our suggestion is that you bring them in from the boardroom and into regular conversations you have with your team members. Their success is partly but not wholly your responsibility – another acre in the territory that goes with the role of the 3$^e$ leader. It's not all carrots, however. . . .

## What are the consequences of failing to deliver your part of this project?

Just as important for some people as reward is the concept of consequences. We know the world is made up of a rough 50/50 split of people in terms of attitude to motivation. About a half have a "toward mentality" that makes goals key motivators. These people see reward and getting the goal as the critical motivator in the way they respond to life's challenges. The other half is made up of "away mentality" people who fear negative consequences more than they value reward. So, they find energy on challenges to avoid the pain and consequence of failure. Given this well researched fact of the human condition, if you use both elements in your commitments actions, then you've nicely hedged your bets.

What we mean here isn't making open threats; it's more a clear and honest explanation of what would happen if they couldn't meet their targets, its effects on the implementation plan, the other team members and on the organization's aims. Again, being explicit about what's expected and why, is the key to getting real engagement and you don't have engagement until you have clear commitments from all of your key players. So carrots need sticks to dangle from.

Nine questions to ask about your ability to clarify and set **Commitments**:

- Are my team members clear about what is expected of them?
- Do my team members know exactly what support I can give them?
- Does each team member have a written development plan with specific targets?
- Do I know where each team member is against target?
- Do I regularly agree targets with individuals?
- Do I encourage ambitious development goals for people and follow up on them?
- Do I keep my commitments to other people inside and outside the team?
- Are consequences and benefits clear to people who work with me?
- Do I provide specific rewards for individuals rather than the same broad brush for the whole team?

We've come across many leaders who are unable to engage their teams and employees, but at times a particular strength can also be overdone. Is it possible to create so much loyalty and commitment locally that it can have wider negative implications for the entire organization and that eventually back-fires locally? Short answer: Yes. Henri was one such leader met in the course of our work.

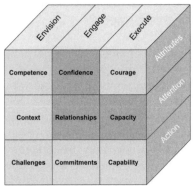

## A cork in a corporate bottleneck

*Henri was the long standing general manager of a sales and marketing organization based in one of the smaller countries of continental Europe. He was effectively the MD of the business, but the structure of the organization meant that his internal title was General Manager. The business that Henri ran was part of a global consumer electronics organization.*

*The role of a country head was to lead the development of the country market across a range of professional and consumer electronics products, whilst supporting European sales and marketing strategies. In real terms this meant growing market share in two distinct industries, one being the more specialist broadcast and professional users buying high value very customized products, and the other being the mass market home consumers.*

*Henri was a professional sales person who believed in the need for a leader to be seen to lead his team. He was considered a very proud man, who had risen through the business on the basis of hard work and good results. Henri was regarded in high esteem by his country management team and at all levels within his organization. However, by his colleagues in the European center and in the regional management team, Henri was seen as arrogant and self centered. He was sometimes referred to as a big chief in a little country. What couldn't be argued with was his performance in terms of business results.*

*You can see from the diagram that Henri is a competent leader in terms of the model. He is rated after assessment as having strengths, in six of the nine aspects of leadership. The other three are satisfactory. Overall it suggests a strong profile and as already stated he got the results for his part of the business. However, it's only by getting some more detail about each aspect that you can understand why there were still some problems and implications for the organization.*

*When Henri was setting his mid term plans for the business he would spend a lot of time interpreting this with his senior team. He was a shrewd business man who understood the dynamics of his industry within his region. Although not so interested in the wider European business situation he was very aware of what his customers would want and how to grow his market based on this. This gained him a lot of respect from his team, who found him always up to date and informed about the marketplace.*

*He believed that their targets and challenges should be clear and linked to their customer's needs as well as the business. This ability to provide clarity of the link between what challenges the company faced and the actions that he wanted his team to take meant little was misunderstood in his team. He used this very practical approach to ensure that all members of his team then cascaded this understanding down. In short Henri was good at Envisioning and helping people grasp the new business challenges they faced. Henri believed that to get good performance, all the employees needed to know the company challenges, the targets that the business was aiming for, and crucially why these targets were important.*

*His immediate team members were given clear commitments of support from Henri, and very clear commitments were expected in return. The regard he was held in by his local team meant that his advice and coaching was welcomed and his support taken as something of value. He was admired and respected by his own team.*

*In Henri's approach to engaging others there was room for some improvement, however. This statement needs to be put into context. His employees and management team were by any measure fully engaged. In fact, rarely do you see such loyalty and trust as in the employees within this organization. The area that Henri did not pay sufficient attention to was the relationships he had with his peers and his European bosses. In this context his confidence was seen as arrogance. Henri would show openly his dislike for European directives and initiatives preferring to use his market knowledge locally to get things done. What this created was two distinct pictures of Henri, dependent on which vantage point you were observing him from.*

*So you might say, his results speak for themselves. The problem was not apparent and may not become so for months. Henri was not interested in a career in the European Head Office, as his perception of it, and the relationships he had with it were not good. However, from a talent point of view, he was capable of taking a bigger role with more impact on the total business. But, and again it's a major but, this was not going to happen while this perception gap existed.*

*Henri was not afraid to take tough action with people who he believed were not able to do their job. He was not quick to judge though spending his time reviewing performance and coaching improvement where he could. This again created loyalty and respect.*

*In terms of ensuring there was sufficient capacity in the organization, Henri did miss the opportunities that European support could bring, however. In managing the resources day to day he was quite able, but because of his stubborn attitude he did at times miss out on pan European promotions, consumer task groups, research support and talent pool access all of which a better relationship with the center would have facilitated.*

*Finally, his ability to build capability was excellent. He himself was an able coach particularly on the customer relationship elements of the role. He encouraged others in his team of managers to take development seriously for themselves and their team. He ensured a reasonable proportion of the budget was allocated for staff training and development. In this way he demonstrated to his employees that high performance did not come at the cost of development of teams and individuals. As a result in the annual climate survey his organization scored very positively on morale and motivation of individuals. This was not so common across the rest of the European businesses.*

## Organizational implications

*Henri was seen by those who worked with him as an exemplary leader, always having time to discuss but not direct and always delivering by example. Unfortunately, Henri's belief that the leader's focus was with his team and his staff meant that others in the European organization would find his attitude self-important, as he was seen to dismiss European issues that did not immediately impact on his country operation. This led to him being regarded as arrogant at times and not someone with a real future in the most senior ranks of the organization. Potentially, the company was wasting a real talent on a country level role because of peer perceptions, where his performance in both commercial terms and in the loyalty and support his leadership generated was outstanding. He believed that he was not well regarded by those making selection decisions for senior roles within Europe and therefore there was no merit in being visible to them. This misled perception was also a block to his promotion as he was difficult to persuade otherwise.*

*A second consideration was the fact that being only 47 and being the most senior position in the country organization, but not prepared to move on; he was acting as a talent blocker for people coming up the career ladder. The size of the organization made it a low risk but worthwhile development post, growing talent identified in the central talent pools. Yet, Henri was a very tight cork in that bottleneck.*

## 19 Execute

## Best of both worlds

When asked in an interview what was more important, strategy or execution, Jack Welch, the iconic former head of GE, said *"Both."* Doing what we set out to do with the organization is about execution. Doing the right thing is about strategy. There are no *ors*.

Execution isn't an alternative to strategy – it's applied strategy. Jack Welch was right. It's not a choice leaders make. They must do both. What we do know is that the leader's legacy is built on what they delivered – not what they talked about and that to us means that execution is a thing that we should always have in mind. Early on in developing our plans we should always think about the probability of delivery. Can it be done? If so what would it take, who would it take and how can we get it started?

Executing strategy in any organization is rarely achieved in isolation, which means that the way the leader builds and manages his team is critical to success. There's a clear requirement that all is in place, from budget priorities and internal politics to the elements of the corporate religion and information systems. Leadership is about getting things done and leaders will be judged by what they and their team achieve. The re-energizing leader's role in execution is to endure through the challenges of implementation while increasing the capacity and capability of the team. They need to show **courage** and tenacity in the face of set backs while finding the way to maintain **capacity** and the **capability** to deal with them.

## Executing the right things

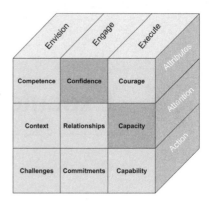

*Sue, a leader of some reputation and record, was and still is a master of execution, heading major restructuring efforts in her organization. The examples given here are of her behavior and situation at a particular point in her career where there were significant challenges to be met. So, this is a historical view of Sue. However, it will be obvious to the reader that many of her qualities are enduring and are still being used successfully today, ensuring that she is in demand in the organization.*

The situation described is a snapshot of the organization and its leadership practices a number of years ago in the growth and expansion stage of a food manufacturing site. This site was the largest manufacturing site the organization owned in its global portfolio. The business across the world employed over 200000 people and operated in almost 150 countries. The site employed 16000 people at one point in history, but now operates with closer to 5000.

Sue is an analytical chemist by training and had come to general management by an unusual route having worked in Human Resources for a number of years, both in staff and factory personnel roles. Sue was considered by many as someone who would listen to the views of others but would need to be convinced of options other than her own. This was not because she was stubborn or intransigent, but more a consequence of her value of logic and need for clear argument was very well developed. This seems to have been a product of her grounding in analysis in her early career as a chemist.

Most of her immediate staff would describe Sue as firm but fair. She was highly respected by her mainly male peers for being straight to the point, and holding strong views based on sound arguments. She could argue her case when she needed to – regardless of the audience.

At one time, Sue was the General Manager of a processing plant in a large food manufacturing site of one of the world's largest food companies. She was responsible for the plant's 24 hour shift working and output. It employed 120 people who were a mix of production staff, maintenance workers and specialists. The task assigned her by the company was to commission, and efficiently run a new manufacturing plant serving several internal customers located across the mainland UK. The continuous supply of the part processed ingredients were to be guaranteed while *maintaining cost effectiveness and the high food safety requirements necessary for this high-contamination-risk food.*

*Sue's profile was a mix of lots of relative strengths and one or two areas with some room for improvement. Most of her profile would be considered very strong. However, both the confidence and capacity boxes would be considered as satisfactory but not outstanding performance.*

*In terms of her ability to envision, Sue was strong in all three aspects. Her background and training as an analytical chemist meant that she had a strong sense of logic and process so she felt comfortable with the detail and operational issues. However, possibly more importantly she was intellectually curious and interested in the wider business issues. Sue was a quick learner and found a means to assimilate what ever she decided was important to her success.*

*Sue's ability to think both wide and deep meant that her ideas were able to be broken down to operational level goals and explained in the context of the factory manufacturing strategy. She could sell a challenge and explain why it was important.*

*Sue was not a soap box speaker, one to rally the troops by large meetings. She was, however, always walking the floor of the production environment, coming in late to shift meetings and early to handovers. In her day to day discussions with her team leaders and production staff she linked what they were doing daily to the wider business strategy. This allowed the people who worked for Sue to always be able to see how what they did mattered and what the effect would be if they didn't meet their department goals. The challenge the new plant faced was clearly articulated to everyone who had an impact on it.*

*A positive strength for Sue was engagement. Yet, as you see in the matrix she has been rated as only satisfactory (mid shaded) on the attribute of Confidence. Sue was able to engage her staff and engender real confidence in her own abilities. She built good relationships with her peers and her senior managers and was well respected. What was missing with Sue was her own confidence in her ability. She was often surprised at how others saw her. Sue would contest feedback if it was too positive. Her self perception was not in line with the perception of others. This made Sue at times suffer from doubt about her own ability. This was not shared by others but something that she experienced when initially taking on projects. She always needed a little time to convince herself she could do it.*

*Her teams were not always easy groups to work with, being both shift workers and production operators. However, Sue's calm and firm style seemed to win their respect very quickly. She was also someone who was able to individualize her reactions and responses, to meet the needs of her teams. So, she did spend time listening to people's concerns and ambitions. From this target setting, work was then able to be carried out in a much more meaningful way than many of her team members had previously experienced. Sue was happy to do deals with people, particularly on career development. Her department had more Open University and MBA students than any other on the site. Correspondingly, she also had the lowest absence and sick rates on site. We think there might be a cause and effect going on here.*

*Execution is what Sue's current success is built on. She may have been respected by her staff and her peers for her style of leadership but her real contribution to the business was getting things done. She could and would take on tough assignments and take hard decisions with people. Sue was someone who wouldn't tolerate fools, although her sense of humor was good. She needed people to do what they said they would do. She would ensure that resources needed to get things done were part of her deal with senior management when she took assignments. In this way, she minimized any capacity issues as early as possible. Her ability to release the capability in people was well known to her peers. Sue managed to balance the need to get things done short term with the need to build talent for the organization. Not many leaders we've worked with do this so effectively.*

*Sue was the safe pair of hands that an organization needs to get sticky projects carried out successfully. She was often used in areas where she had little immediate experience because top management knew she had the capacity to learn and the humility to ask when she didn't know. In a manufacturing environment this meant she was respected for her honesty and willingness to learn from her own staff. Her career is solid and satisfying for her, as one of the most senior female managers in the organization and the most senior in manufacturing sites.*

## 20 Elements of execution

### Strength, courage and wisdom

Execution requires courage. Leaders capable of re-energizing the organization are frustrated with inaction, and therefore show courage by jumping into action, so that things begin to happen. Re-energizing leaders don't hesitate to do the right thing, even if it's unpopular with others or difficult to do. They aren't easily diverted from what they set out to achieve. This isn't just a personal ambition or stubbornness but one that transfers into their work and organizational aims.

Prospective $3^e$ leaders should ask themselves five critical questions and consider if they have the courage to really lead:

- Do I have the mental energy to carry through this challenge?
- Can I take tough decisions when they affect people I know?
- Do I have the strength to change my mind when I'm wrong?
- Do I take measured business risks?
- Can I deliver on my promises no matter what?

Team members admire the courage to stand up and do something and not shy back to the safety net of "more research," seeking wide "blame sharing" constant consensus and general managerial procrastination. People prefer to be led, rather than managed. This courage and personal drive we've seen present in all exceptional leaders we've encountered, regardless of the arena in which they operate. Courage requires large reserves of mental energy. We think it's something that leaders should ask themselves before taking others on the journey. Do I have the mental and physical energy to lead?

Within some organizations, as it is in Sony Europe, courage is written into the competency definitions for leadership. In other companies and organizations it may be expressed differently, but some conceptual representation of drive will most likely be featured in their leadership framework. In many organizations, selecting leadership talent has been a straightforward process of matching talents with tasks. Now, companies should actively look for *positive deviance*, the skills and attitudes that make leaders stand out from the average.

Recognizing drive and personal energy is important as a start. Accommodating it within the organization is another matter. By their nature exceptional leaders stand out, in terms of reputation, in terms of results and in terms of their restlessness. They need a succession of challenges to retain their interest and as an outlet for their energy. So, just as this energy can be driven in the direction of improvement, delivery and execution of big plans, it can if not harnessed become mischievous or cynical. Harness it positively before it bites your corporate behind.

Firm but fair is the epitaph of choice for many people managers. Team members and others in regular working contact with the leader need to know that he/she is fair in his/her dealings but at the same time unwavering. Leading, in contrast to merely managing, requires a clear position on things. Even when the decisions are about people they know well the leader must be able to convey both equality of treatment and at the same time focus on the issues. Firm but fair is the perception that comes with re-energized leadership. Taking people on a journey of change requires that there's consistent and committed leadership and the way people are treated is one very visible example.

If team members who don't contribute or deliver their commitments to the project are allowed to engage in "social loafing" then the motivation of others wanes. Nobody likes to see people getting away with being lazy when they are working hard. Natural human behavior!

A 3$^e$ leader needs to deal with the "will" or "skill" issue behind the lack of performance. These can be tough decisions that many avoid hoping that somehow it will all work itself out. This is a monumental folly of thinking. Ignoring a performance problem with someone because you like them isn't smart. If you want to re-energize your team then at times it will feel like tough love – making tough but right decisions about the people you lead.

## U2

But not all courageous decisions are about others. An equally tough decision to make as a leader is to change your mind and admit you were wrong. Not many people find this easy in our experience and when you're in the public space leaders occupy, not easy at all. Nevertheless, as we've already discussed, leadership requires high levels of confidence, and this mixed with the courage to be humble, will make the ability to change your mind something that's admired and not regarded as a weakness. We're not talking about pin ball machine thinking here. It's not OK to switch direction, goals and tactics like the silver ball in the machine but it's OK to change track when the conditions require it and to explain to people affected why you have to.

All businesses operate with a certain amount of risk and all elements of the business carry some of that risk. We know from economics and commerce that high risk ventures should carry higher returns, just as solid dependable investments return a lower dividend. We believe that leaders who take some risk are the ones that return the real benefit to the organization. When we're taking an organization through the maelstrom of change there's bound to be risk. Making a quick but reasonable assessment of risk means that things can be progressed not stalled waiting for certainty.

Re-energizing leaders seem to have a radar for risk that allows them to navigate with more certainty than most. We see risk-taking, as opposed to gambling, as a core aspect of sound leadership and something that leaders need to feel comfortable and confident with.

Finally, there's the issue of delivery on what you promise. All humans trust behavior over and above rhetoric. What we actually do shows more about our values and commitment than what we say we're going to do. As a leader you're in a position of trust and in many cases you're taking others to places they didn't imagine without your guidance. That places a special responsibility on you to deliver on that vision, that dream you share and particularly on the parts that are your commitments to the individuals you work with. Leading by example is still the strongest motivator of positive performance we know. Remember this when things are messy and it would be easy to give up.

Nine questions to ask about your **Courage**

- Do I stick at what I set out to do, no matter what?
- Am I able to take tough decisions even when they affect people?
- Am I considered to lead by example and not ask others to do what I will not do?
- Do other people see me as someone who treats others fairly?
- Will I take a measured business risk if it's the right thing to do?
- Would peers consider me to have integrity?

- Would my team automatically know I would support them when dealing with senior management?
- Do I change my mind if I am shown to be wrong?
- Do my team members give direct and open feedback on my performance?

## Capacity and capability

The other two elements of execution are capacity and capability. Managing the resources needed to be successful over time requires leadership attention throughout the project or change process. Paradoxically, in the process of executing, leaders actually must be the most hands-off in relation to the task. Their focus of attention is on balancing capacity and capability. They must provide focus and direction. Leaders should ensure that all the necessary resources are available or some creative alternative found, but they shouldn't do the job themselves. If you want DIY then do it at home.

Once again there are critical questions to ask yourself about the capability aspects of the execution of your vision.

- Do I have the right measures in place for this project?
- How is the communication of progress going to be done?
- Do I have any contingency plans thought through?

$3^e$ leaders start to balance capacity and capability by selecting the right measures that allow them to monitor and balance the myriad of resources needed for the change process to be successful. We see most winning leaders use some form of performance dashboard made up of a selected few critical measures. This allows them and, just if not more importantly, the team to see where they are on execution at a glance. These measures are a shared resource and not something used to beat the team up about. In some organizations a methodology like Six Sigma provides the mechanism for such a dashboard, but it's not a prerequisite to use a branded process. The main differentiator between successful dashboards and those used to offer the veneer of control, is the choice of meaningful metrics.

## The performance dashboard

Not everything that should be measured can be measured and not everything that can be measured should be measured. How often in organizations do we measure things because of history rather than utility? Outstanding leaders have such clarity of purpose that it defines their implementation measures to some degree. It seems obvious if you want to improve customer satisfaction that you measure how satisfied customers are directly over time. However it's not uncommon for organizations to take this metric and use an indirect measurement, such as order fulfillment, or average time to installation, which are partial measures and not necessarily directly linked to the critical dimension of customer satisfaction. We have a simple piece of advice; if you want to know what's important to the improvement of a dimension ask the end user and listen to what they say – don't assume you know or use a measure just because you already have it.

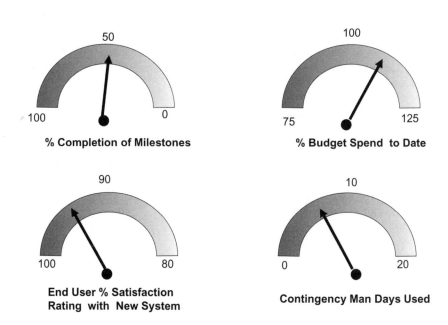

What's important is that the critical few elements are identified, measured, tracked and that the information is used by as many people as possible. Our dashboard is more like the sparse dials on a Ducati GT 1000 rather than the cockpit of a Boeing 767. We want to be able to know what's happening at a glance while moving at speed, not work out what the relationship is between 20 variables, while the machine is on autopilot.

Selecting the right measures will depend entirely on the challenges you're facing and the sort of organization you're leading. What's true in every situation, however, is that there should be some direct connection, or a clear line of sight between what you're measuring and the results you're trying to achieve for the business. Sounds obvious, but we're continually surprised how many businesses measure what they can measure, not what matters. That cosmic accountant Einstein once said: "Not everything that can be counted should be counted and not everything that counts can be counted."

If you need to know the effects that your actions are having on less concrete areas of business like employee satisfaction or customer perception, then there are small scale pulse surveys you can organize using very low cost web based software. You could even push the boat out and actually talk to people in ad hoc focus groups – and gain an insight into your impact.

The important issue to recognize is that the measures used should be linked, in some mechanistic – cause and effect – way to the actions you take. So, increasing an action has an effect on the measure – either direct incremental or inverse incremental. That's how you know you're getting closer to the goal.

## A surprise you don't want – PANIC

Given that you have measures you can monitor the progress of the goals you and your team are delivering against. But what about when the dials shout at you PANIC!

With a few notable exceptions, contingency planning is something that seems to be the reserve of civil emergency coordinators and not a regular aspect of managers in business. Why is this? We see many great managers and some fine leaders of teams neglect the ideas of downside planning or risk assessment on their goals. In many cases this aspect of capacity management is the differentiator between those that deliver regardless of "unforeseen problems" and those whose projects crash and burn. The trick to avoiding unforeseen problems is to foresee them! At least engage the brains of your team to think about what could go wrong and capture this thinking somehow. To be prepared is to be forearmed. Given a team of bright people it's not that difficult to predict 80% of the issues that could occur on the execution of the project. We suggest that this part of the capability planning is taken seriously and that likely risk is assigned to each element. At the best, it will unveil some hidden threat in enough time to avoid it ever happening. At the very least, it will be a fantastic opportunity to explore the project time line with the whole team.

**Bright Idea No. 4 – Group Mind Mapping Creative Contingency Plans**

Group mind mapping is a method to both explore future opportunities and to do some creative risk assessment/contingency planning.

Most people have come across the concept of mind mapping – using symbolic and free form connected maps of situations rather than linear notes or schematic diagrams. They are great tools for collating and creating contingency plans. Remember the core, short phrases or words, icons, links, speed and ordered chaos reigns in mind mapping.

Ask each team member individually to brainstorm in color the issues, targets, delivery plans that you're trying to get to. The challenges you've articulated should be the center of these mind maps and related issues radiating off them. "Individual first – shared second" is the most productive way of doing this from our experience and from research evidence on how our minds work.

When all the issues affecting the plan are laid out, ask the individuals to share their plans, to build a central mega map of the challenges your team face. This is another sharing process – not on creating the plan but on delivery. Then, get them to actively be devil's advocate – put on the map, everything that could go wrong, if the worst happened. Be creative and focus on all the arms of the map – if it could go wrong what would it look like?

Then, take a break, have a coffee, a walk in the park or even if time allows on your schedule sleep on it. The brain, even in exciting company, benefits from some downtime to process. You also need time to switch mental models from disaster prediction to disaster recovery. When you start again to take a second bite, take real pride and passion in removing the obstacles, by examining, predicting how you'll deal with the issues, and managing the contingency. Solve the unforeseen by foreseeing them and dealing with them. Most of what appears unpredictable in your change processes can be predicted if you only try – test it out – what have you got to lose?

Managing capacity also comes down to having clear priorities. If every-thing is important – nothing is important. Have you ever had too much to do on your to do lists? The old adage "If you want something doing give it to a busy man will only go so far". Tear up the current to do list and replace it with this alternative approach to time management.

---

### Bright idea No. 5 – Not to do Lists

Capacity is about time as well as activities. Plans, measurements, charts, contingencies and problem solving all take that most valu-able resource – time. How do you practically free up time to do the right things? We want to save you from the tyranny of time by sharing with you a counter intuitive but useful exercise. Re-energize your efforts by focusing on just the things that matter – start a *not to do list*. Do it today.

How often do we attend meetings or workshops and come away with great long lists of things to do that we've either learned, or somehow knew already but have been refreshed in our minds. The reality of this is that we then return to our desks, office or laptop to find out that the world has missed us and there are demands on our time to catch up on.

What happens to the extra stuff on the "to do list"? It invariably suffers as we realize all the extra things to think about and do. Also at the individual level, exploitation crowds out creation. We encourage people to create "not to do lists". Free up time by removing less productive actions, less critical meetings, less impor-tant reports, less interesting people from your day.

If you think about the process it's a critical evaluation of your time management and a positive decision to change what you do by not doing something. We find they are revealing exercises in sorting the chaff from the wheat of the daily workload and are also easier to implement.

---

Nine questions to ask about your ability to manage **Capacity**:

- Can I be innovative about securing resources to get something done?
- Will I always follow up on actions agreed in meetings?
- Will I call in favors from my network to meet a deadline?
- Do my peers consider me a good project manager?
- Do my team members know exactly where they are against plan at any time on a project?

- Have I defined multiple measures of progress and success for each project I undertake?
- Do my plans always include a contingency element?
- Do I make sure that financial implications are always clear?
- Will I bring in resources from outside the team to get results?

## Do you have the capability?

While capacity is about time and resources, capability is about talent and motivation. Re-energizing the organization is as much about regeneration of capability as it is about increasing energy. If the people who joined your organization are only using the same skills and abilities as when they joined then be scared – your organization's life is limited. Orchestrating the capability mix in your team is the conductor's role – getting the best sound from the available instruments, and keeping the whole thing in time.

Ask yourself:

- Are you someone who enjoys developing talent?
- Can you delegate with confidence and not get sucked in?
- Do you coach rather than instruct your people?
- How good are you at giving and receiving feedback?

We believe there are two capability roles for the leader: orchestrating what you have now and finding/nurturing the next virtuoso players. Let's start with getting the best performance from what you have now.

The $3^e$ leader is constantly tracking the motivation and mood of the team. It's our personal experience, and that of leaders we talk to, that when a group of people take on a significant project or business challenge over a period of time the morale and energy ebbs and flows. Human beings aren't machines that tick and hum to a constant rhythm set by the chief engineer. We're a bit more complex and respond to external pressures and successes in different ways. When teams perform in sync it's a pleasure to lead; when team members perform dysfunctionally as a collection of misled individuals it's painful to observe.

As the leader you have the responsibility to keep the team as close to sync as possible and that requires you know what a well balanced and high performing team feels like. Building this capability to maintain high performance over time is a leadership role. Your actions and choices will depend on the size, experience, geography and technical specialism. Virtual and dispersed teams need as much, if not more, communication as intact and in place teams, but the logistics are more complex to achieve. Cross functional teams have different requirements in skill building and flexibility of working than core teams of similar experts. What we both know from experience is that you must devote time to continually taking a pulse of the team, to know as early as possible when there's a symptom of uncertainty, stress, discontent or anxiety about their task. Thinking of this as some sort of energy radar is helpful – scanning for blips on the horizon – seeking out what's incoming, rather than responding to the emergency of impact.

Strategy execution is further energized by leaders boosting the psychological capital of others, and letting them experience success while providing feed-back swiftly and face to face. One of the most effective and actually efficient ways of doing this is through smart delegation of authority. We say authority pointedly, as many managers see delegation as a quick route to getting rid of the grunt work in their in tray and not as devolving real responsibility to both develop others but also increase overall capability in the team or department. They do more meaningful work and you do less work that could be better resourced by your team.

Finding the right talent to lead the business, as a whole or in part, is the defining challenge for organizations today. With the right leader in the right place at the right time the business will thrive, not just survive. There's plenty of evidence in the business press to show the contrary. Capability development is therefore a major element and critical action for the effective leader. We mean the practical development of talent, not just the sponsoring of the corporate graduate recruitment process. We're more concerned with the day to day processes of delegation and coaching that develops people on the job in a practical way. It's a case of teaching people to fish expertly rather than handing out more sardines – help to self-help.

---

### Bright Idea No. 6 – Coaching as a Beautiful Game

Many of the people we've worked with consider themselves as quite able to coach, but often we see them instruct others or offer solutions rather than coach people. When we talked to a number of them and dug into why coaching seemed too artificial and instructing seemed OK, their explanations boiled down to how awkward they felt about following a particular coaching process or framework. As one senior manager told us "they know when I'm trying to coach them and I feel as though it's a bit false when I know from experience the answer to their problems. . . . It's almost like I'm playing a game of coaching, and both know the rules, my move next." Wow . . . what a revelation on reflection. What's wrong with treating it as a beautiful game! Enjoy coaching, getting people to realize their potential, not show them our expertise. Do you think a Premiership coach tells people exactly what to do when they are on the pitch? No, it's impossible. What they can coach is choices and options.

In this case we coached John to enjoy what he was good at but felt guilty about doing. He knew that coaching required him to ask good questions, not provide all the answers. He knew it was about helping others find choices that they select from. He knew it was about getting them to that Eureka-moment in their thought processes not telling them what to do. What John didn't know was that the internal smile he got when people progressed from one level of uncertainty to one of choices and possibilities was OK!

Think of coaching as a mental game. It doesn't matter if the other person knows you're playing the coaching game if your intent is to build capability and there's nothing wrong with enjoying seeing it succeed. Ask Liverpool's Rafael Benitez.

## Dining on feedback

Feedback is, we're told, the breakfast of champions. How much real feedback do you give and encourage in your people? Again, it provides you an ideal opportunity to lead by example. Feedback is a skill that can be learned but the will to give it has to be there in the first place. The most important element isn't the process, the feedback sandwich, the precise nature of the examples but the intent to assist and help the person you're offering feedback to. The rest is minor and can be learned but the intent to help others see what they may not be able to see isn't something that can be faked. Open and sincere feedback is a great way of developing the people who work with you.

In working with organizations on the development of their staff, the most underrated and least used tool in the tool box of leaders seems to be that of feedback. During college and school we get regular updates on our progress, grades and percentage scores of our work. These tell us how we're doing and if we're getting better or worse. When we start work and enter our careers it seems that the need to know the score stops, and specific helpful comments in the margins disappear. We know that if this is re-instated, sometimes enormous improvements in the levels of performance and skill development follow. By the way, for clarity, we're not advocating the use of red pens on reports, more the use of specific discussion with an aim to improve.

Nine questions to ask about your ability to build **Capability**:

- Do I set ambitious development goals for people and review progress against them?
- Do I recognize mistakes as part of learning and developing new skills?
- Do I delegate to the best person for the job regardless of their role or seniority?
- Do I have a reputation for attracting talented people to the team?
- Do I regularly spend time in team meetings talking about the team process and not the task?
- Do I give open and honest feedback regularly to each of my team?
- Do I have a separate team development budget?
- Can I identify talent for other parts of the organization?
- Do I regularly discuss careers and ambitions with each of my team?

---

### Bright Idea No. 7 – Rules of Play Day

How often have you joined a new team in your career and it has taken some time to work out who's really who and how things work round here? We've all faced these times and dealt with them as unavoidable parts of joining a team. It's the storming process of becoming part of the group. As a leader you can short cut or at least accelerate this process for everyone (including yourself) by having a Rules of Play Day. It's a day spent on designing the optimum way of working round here for the team you work with. It can be the same team – new challenges, same challenges – new team or new team – new challenges. . . . it doesn't matter, but a day outlining the way the team works together in some format is precious time very well spent.

Research by Bruce Tuckman back in the 1960's showed that teams need to create their own norms of behavior before they can become high-performers. It's as true now as it was then. ROPD accelerates this process, making explicit the nature of being a player in this team.

It can be a facilitated process but in many cases it can be completely self generative. Aim for an output of catchy one line rules of play. The side benefit of this participation is clarity not only about the rules of play but the game itself and the results expected. Help your team play to the same agreed rules and benefit from less refereeing. Know the game, know the players and know the rules – a recipe for successful team working.

---

## The balancing act

By balancing capacity and capability, and placing a light or heavy hand on the tiller when necessary 3e leaders maintain the organization's ability to deliver change. In this way a leader's role has moved from planning tasks and strategies to attracting and developing talent and then deploying resources in the most effective way. It's quite a move from the more popular leadership concepts of "blue sky thinking" and "strategizing." In our experience, successful leaders not only know the value of building capability in others and in effectively managing capacity, but also take on the personal responsibility to do it. Capacity isn't something for corporate planning and capability isn't the realm of human resources alone, it belongs to the remit of the leader.

You can see why if drawn into the details of day to day delivery or hands-on micro management they will not have time or energy to manage the key to execution, the balance of capacity and capability. To succeed, re-energizing leaders must set time aside to transform, not only perform.

One of the executives we coach, Tony, is the head of a very successful niche recruitment organization. They have in their few years of business won repeated industry awards for their customer service and approach. His energetic and hands-on approach to business ensured that attention to detail and sales focus were the two operating principles of his firm. In a competitive industry they have carved out a very nice position punching well above their weight. Tony had a major injury a year or so ago and needed to stay away from the office and let his body repair. On getting the all clear from his medic he returned to the business to find chaos, and the worst six months of results the company had ever had. He thought his team members were leaders, but in reality he only had followers of his instructions. Tony talked to us and reflected on his team's efforts without him. He resolved to develop leaders who could run his business and let him concentrate on strategy and expansion.

However, the stranglehold of success exerted its pressure again, and during the next year Tony delayed his leadership development program to chase short term results and awards. Three times he delayed their workshops, in the same timeframe losing key members of his team. Will he ever be able to let go of the operational reins and get more strategic? Time will be his judge. DIY business should be left to people putting up shelving, not building an empire.

Strategy execution is about turning challenges into change by implementing the plan. Sounds like a statement of the obvious. Yet, if you have a plan agreed upon – a plan that your team and others necessary to make it happen are committed to – then execution is about implementation. This means that the leader's focus is on resource management or building capacity and people management, which is about capability and talent development.

## 21 In the army now

### Taming "Tommy"

To further increase your understanding of the $3^e$ model let's examine one of the most respected and successful institutions in the world; the British Army. Observing the popular external image and impression of the Army it would be hard to imagine an organization that epitomizes leadership more. When other nations apply brute force or "shock and awe," it's often the British Army that leads the world in intelligent defense and measured tactical response. As a leadership brand, the British Army has an enviable record. However, being outstanding at what you do doesn't make you immune to social and political change. When your environment and the talent pool you recruit from has evolved into something quite different from your historical fishing grounds, then as an organization you need to stand to attention.

Now, let's be clear at this point that we're not saying the British Army is a typical organization, but as an example of what change does to the leadership requirements of the business it will illustrate our point nicely.

We know that the Army has some restrictions on its operational model, or its business processes. This is an organization that can't outsource its core activity – at least not outside of traditional relationships such as the Ghurkha regiments. Given this major difference to the commercial world, the Army faces a challenge that commercial solutions can't help them with.

Even organizations built on strict need for discipline and clear lines of command, such as the British Army, have to face the emerging change in the collective mindsets of potential and current employees. What used to work in the past no longer meets requirements. At the raw recruit level they have two problems. One they know how to deal with and have a plan for. For the other one, none of this is currently true.

It seems the basic raw material for an infantryman or field soldier is no longer playing sport as often, as active as previous generations or having as healthy a diet as their parents had. The "PlayStation generation" as journalists and Army insiders have dubbed them, need to be pre-conditioned before entering basic training. A new three week pre boot camp program has been designed to try to give the new recruits a higher chance of passing the 12–14 week basic training.

Personal fitness, problem one, solved in age old Army style: Half rations and double duties. However, the second problem the PlayStation generation has set them isn't so easy to resolve.

The Army has a long and noble history of leadership and is respected as one of the most capable fighting forces in the world. However, the British Army is now realizing that new recruits to the ranks find the nature of absolute subservience a real culture shock. If we think about it, it's likely that the people who consider being a full time soldier in any force must have considered that they would need to follow orders. So, we think it shouldn't be a surprise to them when they are asked to do as they are told. Yet, the military's own occupational psychologists and researchers at one of Europe's leading business schools have found clear evidence that today's recruits, even though expecting this regime, find the reality a true culture shock. It's just so alien to everything they are experiencing in the real world they have grown up in.

This new reality is one that the Army is finding difficult to deal with. It seems to us that, outside of a few religious orders and none of them could be called growth industries, nowhere else in modern society is unquestioning loyalty and obedience routinely expected from employees. The Army's experience is that new recruits just don't react to orders in the same way that recruits have for the last 40 years, yet the demographics of the applicants have not changed significantly, just the general societal view of blindly following orders without knowing why. We've come to the conclusion that the *why* question is a critical one for modern working man.

We have found in discussions and research that this need to know why doesn't stop with 17 and 18 year old new recruits. The Army is having significant problems recruiting the officer material they need to lead the Army now and in the future. It appears that the values of duty and public service aren't held in as high a regard as in many previous generations of potential recruits. Bright young graduates are much more likely to be excited by a career in McKinsey or Microsoft than by the genuine risks and evident hardship of the Army. The unquestioning loyalty demanded from a Queen's commission, and the restrictions that the lifestyle places on young potential officers has made recruiting at this level a real problem. Either the quality of applicants isn't high enough or the necessary numbers just aren't attainable. The combination of low quality/quantity officer material and rank and file recruits with cultural and psychological issues isn't one that can be ignored. Add to this situation another element of their culture – you don't recruit into senior ranks. It's simply not allowed.

All of this is happening at a time when the role that they play, the core mission of the organization, is at a level of demand that has not been seen for 50 years. The knock on effect of recruitment problems is that the organization is calling on its reserve forces. These are a part time selection of bank managers and warehousemen who take up the uniform a few weekends a year for an annual bonus-earning two week camp. Not a great state of affairs for one of the world's premier fighting forces to be in.

So, here is an organization with a long history of success, they have not lost a war/conflict in 100 years, yet they are being forced to reappraise the style of leadership they apply. They recognize that the current doctrine and approach, while effective in a conflict, doesn't deal effectively with all the other situations that they find themselves in. More importantly, if they can't evolve their style to one that's both effective and attractive to the modern thinking recruit, then they may find that they can't maintain the numbers and quality of people they need to respond to the call should it come, something they call Force Elements at Readiness (FE@R). We can only hope they find a way to square this circle.

# A call for action

If an organization with a reputation like the British Army has to rethink and reflect on its style of leadership, with its history of success in command and control, then think what organizations without such a doctrine of discipline would need to do.

We believe that the harsh truth of the matter is that bright and talented people do not just do as they are told anymore. You may of course be in an organization that only hires stupid people (yourself excepted), but today these are few and far between and those that do so are destined to be taken over or become a casualty of consumer choice in the short to mid term. Even the lowest skilled roles are becoming the focus of re-engineering to make them more "added value" and therefore in many ways more demanding. What we do know is that talented people also need great organizations in which to shine.

So *how* do you lead people who demand more from their leaders?

We can see the effects of boredom and blind "followship" on retention in many of the service center roles created as part of the growing online self service culture. For many new graduates in the UK and many parts of Europe, their first employment position is working within a call center or some other form of repetitive service role. In many of these jobs you're asking educated people to work in ways that demand lots of compliance and procedure following. At some point they will ask why they are doing this, and if you don't, as an organization, have an answer, first the discretionary effort disappears then the motivation to do even the basics quickly follows. The need for earning money is a clear incentive for first job applicants, but it neither retains them nor motivates them to produce their best.

If we accept that leadership is a high level skill and an ability that organizations value, then we need to understand what it is that constitutes leading. In proposing our model of $3^e$ leadership we're clear that the primary purpose of leading is to deliver organizational outcomes. For most organizations this takes the form of change – preparing for the future rather than managing the present.

What we see is different from most models of leading is that there's a clear link between the need to clarify vision, get people engaged in the process and finally execution. Our approach is both a **why** and a **how**. We believe that to lead others through change you need to help them answer why and also to ensure they know how. We also believe organizations that do this will attract talented people who need to feel valued. Double whammy – you lead better change processes and you get better people into the organization.

Many other attempts to define an approach to leading concentrate on specific aspects of leading without reference to the purpose, getting things done. Results in business are pretty much everything and leaders are the people who have the most influence on getting them. As David Ulrich, the recognized *uberguru* of human resources, unequivocally puts it: "Effective leaders get results."

# 22 How to develop leaders

## In the beginning there's talent

Our approach to finding or selecting those individuals with the highest probability of being successful is based on core attributes or core competencies. Many organizations have competency frameworks developed for them by experts in job assessment or internal HR teams. We think these should be primarily focused on the leadership pipeline and used to select talent, those positive deviants with an above average propensity to lead.

Remember the critical questions we asked you to consider in Chapter 16:

- Is the person smart enough to understand the business, at both the strategic and operational level?
- Do they have the ability and confidence to build strong relationships with people at all levels?
- Are they driven to make things happen for themselves and for the business?

What would be the answer if you posed those questions to yourself or your team? If you can answer positively the above questions about the leaders in your business then they probably have a reasonable threshold level of the core attributes needed. They should be above average in the intellectual and psychological dimensions, and they should possess a higher than average drive or motivation to act – positive deviants.

When an organization agrees with us and decides that this approach is useful to them, then it's actually a relatively straightforward process to screen your management or leadership population for those with the highest probability of making exceptional leaders. This is a highly skilled activity even though it appears to be a simple process. Just as in sport, the real experts – from Cristiano Ronaldo to Ronaldinho – make the difficult look so easy. A robust system of assessment isn't so hard to create but its rigorous application requires a little more courage and ability.

We're clear in our minds that this $3^e$ leadership approach will only be used if it makes sense to business people, not just HR managers or consultants making a living from assessment. When creating the model it was important that it was robust and research based and that it was focused on what makes the difference between exceptional leaders and the rest. It's possible, we know because we do, to use the above questions with any sales manager or engineer and determine from the responses they give, whether the staff that they employ in their business have the potential to be leaders. When you get that look of doubt, then we know there's more work to do on selection.

It's true that some in the human resources field find this idea of selective talent abhorrent and in some people's eyes it's élitist. They prefer to support the idea that talent is everywhere and in everyone, and the role of talent management in organizations is to reveal the hidden talents of every employee. While we're all talented, our belief is that when it comes to finding leadership talent, that approach is like spread betting, investing a little in many pots and hoping that the development of one talent will offset the cost and time lost on the many. Actually, the real value comes from identification of leadership talent, and then feeding it like a prize bloom, not spreading the fertilizer scattergun-like hoping something will thrive. The research evidence is clear that re-energized HR strategies can and do add value to the organization.

What's now becoming clear is that the focus on differentiated strategies in reward, development and retention is the way to really enhance business performance, something that one size fits all approaches fail to do. We advocate finding those in your organization, or outside it, with real positive strengths and build on those pluses. Add to what people are already good at and ensure they apply their strengths – don't force them to focus on what they aren't good at, as some form of development path. There's now a growing realization amongst some of the more enlightened companies to allow people to build on the success they already have.

Sony Europe is one such organization. It has re-invented its appraisal system and development thinking to focus on individual strengths. This isn't as simple a process, as reviewing and altering the paper work associated with appraisals, but more about the evolution and behavioral change of the leadership and management of the organization.

Our view is that leadership skills can be developed, but also that organizations are far better off starting with good material in the first place. This requires that the guardians of talent, the HR professionals, shouldn't shy from the task of assessing people, but should find accurate and transparent ways of defining and selecting for leadership positions. If you concentrate on people who have the propensity to lead and take the challenge of change, then you're gambling with more certainty and better odds. Working with these strengths and positive framework makes leadership development as much about deployment as it is about education. We go back to the mantra: the Right people + the Right place + the Right time.

## The lack of leaders

Not everyone who could lead wants to lead. It's a tough task in most organizations and the demands that leadership places are too great a price for some people. With the emergence of the downshifting phenomenon among some of the most successful people we should recognize that not everyone is driven to lead and take the challenge of changing an organization. A second thought is that those who have that drive may not always want to apply it forever in your business.

$3^e$ leadership recognizes this aspect of human nature. Not all the intelligent and capable people who could lead choose to act out their leadership potential. Either they aren't interested or motivated to act, and incredible to some of us, sometimes too lazy to take the task on. So, in the shorthand of $3^e$ leadership, they have the competence and confidence but not the courage to act.

Equally, you can have people who are truly driven and can strive towards stretch targets while uniting their team towards a goal. But ultimately they spend their time and the team's efforts on the wrong thing because they lack the intellectual competence to select the right strategic imperative. Again, this can be expressed in the shorthand of $3^e$ leadership as confident and courageous but not really competent.

Finally, as attributes are considered, the impact of confidence shouldn't be understated. In terms of how it manifests itself in a leadership theory, confidence is related to how the person views himself and how others see them. It's about having that air and presence that makes people want to follow you. It's the confidence that inspires others to want to give their discretionary effort. The word "give" in this context is carefully chosen as it's not something that can be taken even by the most manipulative and intelligent of managers. That's why being a person capable of inspiring others, so that they give what's in their power to withhold, is what leadership is really all about. When we're leading others, as John Kotter puts it, "through the struggle of change" then the view that the team holds about your confidence is a critical factor.

## Johan – sinking not swimming

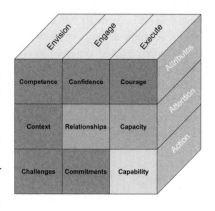

*Johan was one such man who lost his team's confidence. Yet, he was trying to run a major region of a large technology organization. Johan was a likeable successful senior sales manager who had been promoted in the past on the basis of service and sales success in his own country, of which he retained sales head status. He was regarded by his colleagues as being "old school" and loyal but not innovative or driven. Johan was not considered to be someone who would change things or challenge the existing status quo. He seemed to be out of his depth in many meetings in Europe.*

*The European organization was asking for change and results to improve, suggesting radical action was required. Johan was not a strategic thinker and lacked the respect of his team, many of whom thought they had better ideas but believed that they were not listened to. He did not have the confidence of his country heads. His region's results were poor month on month and regardless of the center bringing this to his attention, Johan failed to take action when it was clear some dramatic action was required. Eventually his peers and senior managers ran out of patience and he was sidelined so a more courageous manager could take over the region. Within six months of his replacement being made the region returned to profit and making its budget forecast.*

## Things can only get better

It's difficult to learn to be significantly more intelligent, in the way it's defined in the 3$^e$ leadership approach and no amount of management skills training programs will provide it. Research says that adding a few percentage points onto your IQ is possible over time and with the right environment, but the biggest influence is still in your genes. So, does that mean the majority of us can't lead? The short answer is: No. We believe that there's an opportunity to use the intelligence you have in a more focused way. You can't learn to be a genius, but you can learn to make the most of what you have. We've shared with you some of the tools that any leader of change should have in their kit bag. Using tools to involve others, explain concepts, analyze problems and monitor progress is the way to use your intelligence in a positive way and in a way that demonstrates leadership.

Consider again the issue that not everyone wants to lead. Organizations on the whole tend to promote people into management based on the "Peter Principle", so that the successful sales man becomes the next sales manager, then gets promoted to the regional sales manager and so on. At some point they reach the level of their own incompetence in a discipline that's called leading. They would probably be great sales people if they didn't have to get caught up in the day to day management of people and internal politics that they never envisaged nor wanted when they joined the organization.

A lesson business should learn, but somehow is reluctant to, is that not everyone wants the responsibility of leading a business or a team. Leadership isn't something that turns everyone on. There are many engineers of our acquaintance, both classical old school engineering and the cyber space type, that loathe having to interact with others and take responsibility for them, while relishing the pressure that goes with intricate system diagnosis and problem solving. Our thinking is that it's fine and not something to worry about, unless of course when you recruit such individuals expecting great leaders of people rather than great innovators of systems. As one of the less politically correct IS managers we work with has commented, "giving a great 'code monkey' people to manage is not smart and they hate it." He considers that his job, as the guardian of the IS workforce, is to use this person's talent to the best effect, while valuing what they contribute. He may be regarded by some as a code monkey but by allowing him to do his best work he was earning more peanuts!

## Nurturing nature

One of the biggest debates in history is the nature versus nurture dilemma of psychology. Are we born with genetic predetermined factors of our being or does the environment make us learn and adapt? It's clearly a bit of both but a lot can be achieved by focused and well informed development activities.

John Adair, the elder statesman of leadership, who once lectured at Sandhurst Royal Military Academy, the British Army Officer school, tells a great story about this prickly issue. He smiles when he talks of an NCO, non commissioned officer, who was responsible for some of the basic training of the bright young things at the academy, who when asked if officer cadet Smith was a natural born leader, replied briskly "not yet sir, not yet."

Leadership can no doubt be developed. If you want to become a better leader you can do many things both in the way you approach business and more importantly in the way you lead people around you. We've outlined some of the techniques we've used when working with individual leaders and with leadership teams but there are of course always more ways you can develop.

The big question is how do you know which of the nine areas of the $3^e$ model you're already doing well in and which are the ones to work on?

There are two things that matter – your own perception of how you measure up to this framework, and the perception of the people you work with, or lead.

The most obvious method by which to find out more is to use some form of audit for your self perception and then get this checked out by collating the views of the people you work with and lead. We have developed the tools for you to do this and include the self assessment version at the back of the book. This short inventory will allow you to self rate against a standard five point scale your own ratings on critical aspects of leadership that exemplify the $3^e$ leader.

The results of the self assessment will give you a profile somewhat like that we've shown in the book when giving examples of leaders who we work or have worked with.

If you think of the diagrams we've used to date, the 3D box matrix, the shaded coding system has been used to show relative strengths of each person against the model.

The darkest shading is an area of concern. Mid-grey shading shows satisfactory levels of this element and light shading shows a relative strength. The darker the shading, the more the area is a concern. Those people who show the darkest shading in a box will have difficulty getting that to light up. The people, who showed mid-shading in a box, could with some focused development move this over time to light. As we see from many aspects of positive psychology, and some of the work started by Marcus Buckingham and Donald Clifton building on strengths, if you want to become a peak performer it's smarter to grow plusses than to focus on dealing with weaknesses. So, if you're not naturally strong on linking strategy to concrete goals, in some way lack the abstract thinking and analysis ability then this might be something you need help with, to get it to a hygiene level, or you may want to link up with someone who's great in that particular dimension. Yet, working tirelessly to improve a negative aspect might be a poor development path. Instead, we would recommend you work on the areas of leadership where you show a natural strength or have developed a way of doing well already.

# Profiler

There are three aspects to thinking about your profile or that of others. The attributes of Competence, Confidence and Courage, are seen as critical to the application of leadership. The focus of attention on Context, Relationships and Capacity, are seen as the enablers of change. The actions taken to define the Challenges agree the Commitments and build Capability in your people.

We think some of the attributes that you need to lead should be present at least to a certain level, a sort of threshold of effectiveness. We know from experience, and sometimes painful experience, that some people much as they want to lead don't possess the necessary base levels of intellectual, psychological and social raw material.

If we look at the three attributes that matter in selection of leadership talent in the organization, Competence, Confidence and Courage, there are a number of possible mixes and consequent development issues. All the re-energizing leaders we've worked with or assessed have had these core attributes to an acceptable level, the threshold. It seems from our experience that you need a threshold level of each to make an outstanding leader, and preferably you should be great in one or more attributes.

Someone with this mix demonstrates high confidence, high courage and moderate competence, shown by their profile line overlaid onto the target. There would be a tendency for this profile to lead to some mistakes and wasted efforts because of the likelihood of time and energy being spent on the wrong things. Given their ability to build relationships and their own drive and resilience they could be seen as positive leadership models, but doing the wrong things too many times could ruin their chances of succeeding. In short we could say, good with people, driven to get things done but not the smartest bear in the woods.

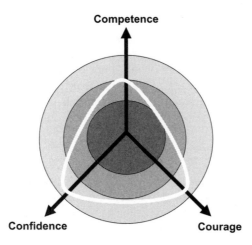

Now, the critical question is; can this profile be developed? Again, if we follow the strengths ideas, we would say not significantly. If we go back to old school psychology and regard our idea of competence as raw IQ, as noted earlier, agreed wisdom says you can move your IQ score a few points to the positive with work but not significantly so. However, we believe there are things that can be done to improve over time. One development strategy to adopt focuses on how these leaders apply their thinking, rather than their raw mental horse power. So, it might be useful to think about where such persons focus their attention, and the subsequent actions that they take. Given that they score well on confidence, suggesting good relationship skills, they can probably also get others to assist in analytical situations therefore playing to the strengths of others. Getting a clear commitment from a trusted team member on issues where they aren't strong may be their best development route. They can then leverage their own strengths to improve their overall leadership capability.

A great worry would be a dark shading score on competence and low scores on the other two attributes. In this case, our profile holder has threshold on all three, i.e. at least mid-grey in one and light in two others.

Let's look at one more potential profile of attributes. Here, we have someone who's again strong in two attributes but not so hot on the confidence area. So, in our shorthand they are smart and have drive but aren't so good at engaging others and building relationships.

How might this affect others? The most common outcome is that they are driven to do the right thing, almost at any cost. Their lack of people radar means that they miss the signals of tiredness, dissent, anxiety or confusion that their team and others show in the course of their work. Being driven and smart they just plough on, oblivious of the burn out around them. People leave leaders like this because of their solo agendas and relentless pace.

So, can these leaders change their spots? Given that they are smart and much focused on results they can learn people management. They will never become therapists or excellent personal coaches – "humanagers" – but they can learn to do what makes teams work well. This is the benefit of being smart and driven. Such people can often apply themselves to what needs to be done, not only what comes naturally.

There's an old and strange saying in the North of England, home to one of us, and that is: "if it looks like a duck, walks like a duck and quacks like a duck, it's probably a duck." Smart people can learn to waddle and quack and they do because they know it's important to their success.

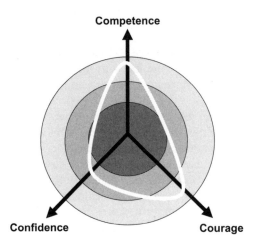

What's often the trigger for these people to learn and change their behavior is the feedback they get from people who matter to their personal perception or alternatively from those who can derail their career. That's where some form of robust 360° feedback process can really make a difference. More of that approach later.

## Re-invent(ory) yourself

When making any investment in development, time or money, you should have a blueprint of where you are and where you want to go to. We've used our experience of working with real leaders in real situations and our understanding of assessment processes to create an inventory for self assessment. The 3ᵉ leadership inventory is a relatively straight forward tool to help leaders get a fix on where they are on the leadership journey.

The inventory is a series of questions about your day to day behaviors that underpin your approach to leading. We've provided a copy of the self assessment element of the full 360° feedback inventory in the later pages of this chapter so you can see how you measure up against being a 3ᵉ leader. The tool is a self assessment inventory designed to assist individuals who are interested in their own development to capture where in the matrix they are strong and where they have work to do. Self assessment requires a certain amount of personal critique and honesty otherwise we just fool ourselves about what we really do and who we are. This inventory is designed to be quite transparent and clear about the issues it's trying to capture. It's not a fully functioning psychometric created to select leaders, but more of a working model for those wanting to develop their own capability as a leader and who seek some guidance to do so.

When you complete the inventory, consider what you do on a regular basis in response to each of the items in the questionnaire. If you only do something occasionally then reflect that to get a true picture of your leadership activity.

To complete the self assessment read each of the items in the list of 45 shown in the table that follows. If the statement applies to you exactly all of the time, rate yourself 5. If the statement doesn't apply to you at all at any time rate yourself 1. The full scale is shown below. Remember 5 if high and 1 is low. Consider not only if the statement is true about you but also how much of the time it's true.

| Does not apply to me | Rarely true of Me | Sometimes true of me | Frequently true of me | Applies to me all of the time |
|---|---|---|---|---|
| 1 | 2 | 3 | 4 | 5 |

Now complete the questionnaire filling in your score for each of the items in the boxes at the end of the item row. Think if you have evidence you could explain to someone else to demonstrate your answer or alternatively if this is something that others could see you do.

| | Inventory Item | Score |
|---|---|---|
| 1 | I make good decisions about people. | |
| 2 | I understand more about my industry than most of my peers. | |
| 3 | I stick at what I set out to do, no matter what. | |
| 4 | I am asked to speak at meetings to give my opinion on matters not my responsibility. | |
| 5 | I am considered to lead by example and will not ask others to do what I will not do. | |
| 6 | I can make good decisions with only limited data or ambiguous data. | |
| 7 | I am trusted with confidential information by my peers and by my boss. | |
| 8 | I enjoy working on complex problems that require new solutions. | |

| | Inventory Item | Score |
|---|---|---|
| 9 | People see me as someone who treats others fairly. | |
| 10 | I can quickly see the crucial issue in any situation. | |
| 11 | I have a good relationship with the senior team and can openly challenge their thinking. | |
| 12 | I will take a measured business risk if it's the right thing to do. | |
| 13 | I understand what needs to be done to make the business better. | |
| 14 | I am happy to admit when I am wrong, even in a group situation. | |
| 15 | Peers would consider me to have integrity in dealing with them at work. | |
| 16 | I have a good network of peers and colleagues inside the company. | |
| 17 | I can be innovative about securing resources in order to get something done. | |
| 18 | My team understands how we make contributions to the wider business plan. | |
| 19 | I meet regularly to talk with my team members about the direction of the business. | |
| 20 | I have multiple measures of progress and success for each project I undertake. | |
| 21 | My plans always include a contingency element. | |
| 22 | I seek feedback from both internal and external customers about our performance. | |
| 23 | When asked my staff knows what the most important business issues are over the next 3 years. | |
| 24 | My staff can see how meeting our challenges also means meeting customer needs. | |
| 25 | I can explain to my team why we're concentrating on specific challenges. | |
| 26 | I am seen by my peers as a good communicator. | |
| 27 | I seek opinions and views from others before taking important decisions. | |
| 28 | I spend a lot of my time talking to people about their work and listen to their ideas. | |
| 29 | My peers would consider me a good project manager. | |

| | Inventory Item | Score |
|---|---|---|
| 30 | I always follow up on actions we have agreed in meetings. | |
| 31 | The goals and objectives of my team address both short term and long term business needs. | |
| 32 | I set ambitious development goals for people and review progress against them. | |
| 33 | I have broken down our overall challenges into operational goals for the team to contribute to. | |
| 34 | I have a reputation for attracting talented people to the team | |
| 35 | Delivery on our goals and objectives will have strategic impact on the business. | |
| 36 | I agree targets with individuals on a regular basis. | |
| 37 | The consequences of failure and benefits of success are clear to all. | |
| 38 | I keep my commitments to other people inside and outside the team. | |
| 39 | I can describe how to overcome the challenges I have set for myself and my team and the benefits of doing so. | |
| 40 | My team members are clear about what is expected of them. | |
| 41 | My team members know exactly what support I can give them. | |
| 42 | I provide rewards and recognition appropriate to individual performance. | |
| 43 | I spend time in team meetings talking about the team process and not only the task. | |
| 44 | I give open and honest feedback to each of my team members on a regular basis. | |
| 45 | I recognize mistakes as being part of the learning and development of new skills. | |

Once you've rated yourself on the items above transfer the results to the table below to reveal the total scores for each of the nine elements of 3$^e$ leadership and where they fit against the benchmark for excellent, satisfactory or cause for concern. So, for competence you would total items 2, 6, 8, 10 and 13 to give your score for this element. To get the score for Envisioning you need to sum the score for Competence, Context and Challenges.

| Element | Items numbers to add together | Total score | E Rating | Totals |
|---------|-------------------------------|-------------|----------|--------|
| Competence | 2 6 8 10 13 | | Envisioning | |
| Context | 18 19 23 24 25 | | | |
| Challenges | 31 33 35 37 39 | | | |
| Confidence | 1 4 7 11 14 | | Engaging | |
| Relationships | 16 22 26 27 28 | | | |
| Commitments | 36 38 40 41 42 | | | |
| Courage | 3 5 9 12 15 | | Executing | |
| Capacity | 32 34 43 44 45 | | | |
| Capability | 17 20 21 29 30 | | | |

Now that you have your individual element raw scores and your totals for each of the E's you can place yourself into the shading system in the table below. So if your total score for Challenges was 20, that would place you in Low-Light meaning that this is a clear strength for you and a part of your leadership you consider you do well. If the total score for Context was 18 this would place you in High-Mid meaning it was satisfactory but could be done better at times or more often.

| Low | High | Low | High | Low | High |
|-----|------|-----|------|-----|------|
| **5–9.5** | **9.6–12.5** | **12.6–15.5** | **15.6–19.5** | **19.6–22.5** | **22.6–25** |

The score you have as a result of completing the inventory shows your perception of your ability as a leader in comparison with the framework called $3^e$ leadership. The items are carefully chosen to represent the day to day activities you do in the normal workplace. It's our actions that demonstrate our leadership not our intentions and our promises. We've emphasized before that it's our behavior that counts not what we say we'll do. This said you've now only gained one perception of that behavior; your own.

Add the scores from your self assessment into the blank elements. Shade it in if you like to see a bolder profile.

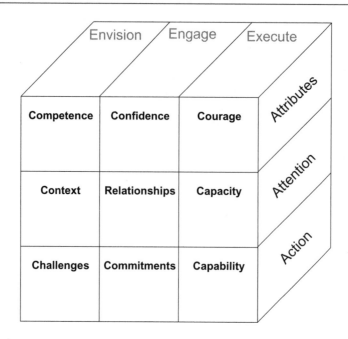

## Bright, Bold and Bored

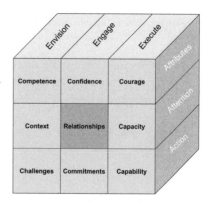

*As part of an exercise in leadership assessment, a large technology business made a rigorous evaluation of all the members in its senior team. This was a brave thing for the HR team and the newly appointed CEO to do. In cases when the team at the top consider themselves the cream that has risen to the top of the milk jug, assessment was never going to be extremely popular.*

*The trick with assessment, particularly with the non-believers, is to make it as rigorous and transparent as possible. Not only that, you must also show that there's a clear business need and case for even starting to consider it.*

*There are generic reasons for needing some form of assessment, such as crisis of confidence in the top team, growth and development for the same, and also for defining the blue print or DNA of leadership. Some reasons are more acceptable than others, but all show a business need and depend on the current results. One or more are applicable.*

*This company not only wanted to code the nature of leadership in the organization (the DNA case), but also aspired for the assessment to reflect the changing demands that re-structuring the business placed on leaders.*

*The method was interview, carried out by respected and expert search consultants, aligned against performance measures in the organization and compared with 360 feedback interviews. The combination of these methods gave a high-resolution picture of the performance of the top executive group, and could then be compared with the market data that the consultants owned. All in all, a rigorous, transparent and demanding process for the participants.*

*What the results told the organization was surprising in many aspects. Of course there was some confirmation of excellence, some agreement where there was cause for concern, but in addition there were some major revelations.*

*In one case the process highlighted a talent, a really intelligent and commercially savvy executive who was battling with a part of the business no one valued and he was getting significant progress. The same executive, Mathias, could see others, not rated as bright or driven, failing in more attractive roles. The results, in from 360°, showed that Matthias's peers found him arrogant and disruptive but all acknowledged that he was very smart. His team found him both challenging and inspiring in equal measure. His boss found him a pain in the butt. Not a good picture so far. However, the search consultants found a bright, bold and bored executive, who felt undervalued and who, frustrated with others not doing their job in bigger roles, became mischievous.*

*The top team made a swift assessment of the talent across the business in Europe and did a double shuffle removing someone for whom the assessment confirmed their fears and gave Mathias a challenge that he wouldn't forget in a hurry. As a non local MD of a failing region with demanding targets and severe re-structuring to do, he would have to expect a rough ride, and that was just in the first year.*

*The epilogue is that within six months, Mathias had engaged his new, smaller team fully. He had a clear strategy in place that they helped build. He needed their local commercial knowledge to do that, and he was smart enough to acknowledge this to his new team. Within these same six months Mathias had turned the corner in the business, returning it to break even from an 18 month decline. He was getting results. He was enjoying contributing again, and for the rest of the organization the removal of his predecessor was a strong positive signal. Since this success Mathias has been given his next big challenge, running a completely new territory outside of Europe. Being bright is good, being bold is good but being bored is a waste of talent and can if not spotted derail the organization.*

# Delighting in feedback

Humans are often blind to what we do well and also what we do badly. Feedback from others, trusted colleagues, bosses, peers, reports and customers is one way to gain a full and comprehensive picture of what really counts, which is how we're experienced by the people we lead.

How often in our family life have we been chastised by our partner for saying something that unwittingly offends someone, or done something that has been misinterpreted in a negative way. We can hear ourselves saying, "but I didn't mean you to take it that way." What counts in communication (and leading others) isn't what we mean but what others interpret from our actions. There's a saying in psychology that the meaning of your communication is the response that you get. No matter what our intent, the meaning of what we transmit is actually not entirely in our control.

360° feedback is now becoming accepted as the principal way to develop an understanding of our effect and affect on others. The two principal ways of getting a full picture of how you lead others are face to face interviews conducted by a trained and experienced third party, and inventory/questionnaire formats. Both have positive and negative considerations and both are worth considering as tools for developing the leader's understanding of the impact he or she has on people. Face to face interviews can provide both the detailed information and the surrounding organizational context to really inform the leader of their strengths and weaker areas. It's, however, both expensive in time and investment. Inventories are less expensive and can provide a good rounded picture of the leader's impact on a variety of people.

The inventory contained in this book is the self assessment version of the 3$^e$ leadership inventory. A full 360° service is available for leaders, and those responsible for the development of leaders, who would like a much richer and more informed picture of leadership.

Much of the development of our effectiveness as leaders comes from changing our actions in response to the feedback we gain from others. The quickest way to improve our performance in any field is to have clear goals, a mechanism for feedback and the wisdom to change behavior to attain an improvement to get closer to our target.

At the very least, the information from a full 360° review is interesting. At the best, it's the trigger for change in the way that people lead that has an immediate affect and effect on the individuals they do lead. The process isn't always comfortable or welcomed by the leaders involved.

Here's the candid response of one participant of such a process in Sony' s European executive team, where part of the model was developed and the 360° feedback was in this case carried out by interview:

*"The assessment interview was a real jolt - suddenly I was 'on the rack', justifying my worth to the company as if I was a new recruit. However, in return, the feedback process was very valuable for me, a real opportunity to reflect on what motivated me and what challenges I need from a business. The peer assessment added hugely to the overall process – it's definitely not comfortable to hear what others think about you, but it can be tremendously valuable if handled well. In the end, what was important was that something tangible happened as a result of the process, both for me and for the business. I'm happy to say that that was the case."*

M.L. Managing Director

Developing leaders requires a clear view of the starting point and a clear target to achieve. In terms of behaviors for excellent leadership, the $3^e$ leadership model provides a framework for both. By self assessment and 360° feedback, individuals can find the areas of strength that they can develop to increase their positive impact, and also identify the areas of concern that they either fix themselves or find another solution to. Again, we go back to the idea that building on existing strengths is the best way to extend your effectiveness, not working extensively on the areas of your profile that are a concern. Fix them by all means, but don't try to turn them into strengths, it's too big a mountain to climb and the view from the top isn't worth it.

We can't prescribe specific development activities for every combination of personal profile. That would be both arrogant of us and incredibly boring for the reader. This development chapter has emphasized the role selection plays in finding leadership talent. Our model suggests that given the right material, competence, confidence and courage the actions of leadership can be learned. Knowing where you are on the development journey is the rationale for the inventory.

What we provide is a robust mechanism for self audit and a clear case for 360° feedback as a tool for development. Using the self assessment tool in this book and the 360° version, available from our website, you can determine in some detail your own profile.

When it comes down to the most effective development process for leaders we believe it's a participation sport and one that for the most part you learn on the job. However, you do need to know the rules of the game and the various game plans to be effective. We've seen some of the best development come from leaders who are given the chance to thrive on the challenge of a stretch assignment. We've also seen well-meaning development managers waste a lot of time, energy and money on sending leaders on badly designed leadership programs. In a participation sport you need to be playing to become better – it's not about learning and not applying – it's about playing to win with a strategy for playing the game.

---

### Bright Idea No. 8 – Three is a magic number

Development is a participation sport. To get it, you need to be doing it. We find that still too many leaders and talented others wait for their HR or line manager to suggest to them development ideas – that's just stupid! Take more responsibility for your development and do at least three things in the next three weeks to make a difference as a result of thinking about applying your leadership capability. We suggest this format, which works with many of the leaders we coach:

- One thing you're going to do differently or better for yourself in the next week.
- One thing you're going to do differently or better for your team in the next two weeks.
- One thing that you're going to do differently or better for the organization in the next three weeks.

---

Sometimes, the most important things are the most difficult to start. Giving a view on other people, assessing talent in others and defining development for team members is something that leaders take as part of their role. We think there's real value also in some serious self-reflection and self indulgent thinking. What about re-energizing yourself? What about re-energizing your own development? The framework we've given here below is a simple and powerful tool for just that. If you do it well, maybe relaxing with a glass of your favorite drink, then it should reveal some of the important but not often discussed aspects of your own leadership. Recognizing your own true ambitions is the starting point in achieving them.

---

### Bright Idea No. 9 – SWAN analysis

Many people have come across the notion of SWOT analysis when thinking about the strategic position of a business. This analysis categorizes business issues into one of four quadrants, Strength, Weakness, Opportunity or Threats.

Not so many people have the discipline to apply this sort of analysis to themselves and their strategic development. The SWAN analysis is a way of applying the same rigor but to the individual and their own development. We've been using SWAN analysis with individuals for some time, and getting great results.

SWAN stands for Strengths, Weakness, Ambitions, and Needs. In this format it's possible to reflect on your own personal qualities and issues and categorize them into some meaningful framework. Having done this, many people feel it helps them with clarity about how and what to develop if they are to meet their needs and realize their ambitions. Sharing our needs with peers and bosses is a logical step after defining them. The more others know about what we need to be successful, the more they can conspire to provide them.

To do this well requires some personal reflection time and some real intrapersonal insight. When complete, the analysis can be part of your personal development route for the next few months or years.

| **Strengths** | **Weakness** |
|---|---|
| What are my personal competencies and qualities that make me stand out? | What are my weaker areas, the areas that I avoid or know I do not enjoy, do well or that don't excite me? |

| **Ambitions** | **Needs** |
|---|---|
| What do I want to honestly achieve in my career, in my life short term? Longer term? | What do I need from the job, from others, from my boss, to achieve my ambitions and feel valued? |

Some of the companies that we work with have taken this applied leadership framework very seriously and designed with us development programs that take high potential candidates, selected by some form of assessment process, and help them learn how to apply their leadership in a day to day manner. The most successful method we use is to define with the business change projects as the development vehicle for the participants. Learning to lead by applying this leadership framework to a real project, with real challenges, real commitments, real capability issues and real expectations of success, is we believe a powerful development experience for anyone who wants to learn.

As one of the greats of organizational development, Kurt Lewin, was reputed to have said: "There's nothing as practical as a good theory." Both of us absolutely support the idea that the real value in theory is in practice and that practice should be supported by a rationale and some real thinking.

We've presented in this book our world view of what it takes to lead in such a way that you and your team can make change happen. It's a particular view crafted from action research, thinking long and hard about success and also reflecting on our 40 years of combined experience of developing leaders with some of the world's best companies.

We passionately believe in the why and the how of change leadership. Continue to work on these two critical dimensions of your own leadership and as you learn to master the art of envisioning, engaging and executing, you'll also realize that:

# Why x How = WOW!

# Index

*Index compiled by Indexing
    Specialists (UK) Ltd*